MY
BEST
LIFE

MY BEST LIFE

An Autobiography by Sakie

——— featuring ———
Traditional & Contemporary Recipes

Valerie Hart

ARCHWAY
PUBLISHING

3 1969 02326 4525

Archway Publishing books may be ordered through booksellers or by contacting:

Archway Publishing
1663 Liberty Drive
Bloomington, IN 47403
www.archwaypublishing.com
1 (888) 242-5904

ISBN: 978-1-4808-1555-1 (sc)
ISBN: 978-1-4808-1556-8 (hc)
ISBN: 978-1-4808-1554-4 (e)

Library of Congress Control Number: 2015903784

Print information available on the last page.

Archway Publishing rev. date: 4/8/2015

About the Author

Valerie Hart, cookbook author (*Bounty of Central Florida, New Tradition Cookbook*), food and travel journalist, Zagat editor and host of the television show, *Back of the House,* teaches cooking to benefit charitable causes. Educated in America, Paris and London, she and her husband, Buddy, manufactured and imported traditional furniture from Italy for three decades. Awarded "Outstanding Woman of the Year" in Miami, she lives in Mount Dora, Florida.

DEDICATION

This book is dedicated to each of us who has loved and been loved by a four-legged soul with indisputable belief in its role in history. Because culinary tastes can also be unilaterally traced directly to historic eras, the protagonists within these pages are depicted as aficionados of gourmet delicacies who share recipes of the times in which they lived.

The world is blessed with a handful of humans who dedicate themselves to the care and safety of animals that cannot care for themselves. One of these caregivers is Katie Hart, a dog trainer, who continually creates more space to accept, feed, and heal castaway cats at her *Hart's Last Chance Ranch*.

For over forty years my life has been fulfilled by talented chefs and writers who dedicate their time and energy toward helping others. It is with apology that I mention only a few.

Alexa Hart Bosshardt - MPS, RDN - Registered Dietitian, Research Chef, and cookbook author with 30 years of experience developing recipes and providing food safety and quality control services to restaurants and food manufacturers. In her 'spare' time, she cycles hundreds of miles to raise money for MS and volunteers at breast cancer fundraising events for both Susan G. Komen and the American Cancer Society.

Carole Kotkin- Manager of Ocean Reef Cooking School, food and travel writer, syndicated food writer Miami Herald, radio host, cookbook author, and my co-editor of Zagat Restaurant Surveys who is never too busy to be my cherished friend.

Chef Jeffrey Rotz CEC, CCE, AAC - Human Resources Consultant/Trainer for the Hospitality Industry Chefs Helping Chefs, President American Culinary Federation Gulf to Lakes Chefs & Cooks Association1996-2014 – Community service leader of chefs and students from Lake County providing "great meals" to the Christian Care Center since 2008.

In Memoriam, Craig Claiborne, my mentor and champion of the amateur cook, who endorsed my first book, *The New Tradition Cookbook*. Craig's dedication to the March of Dimes Gourmet Galas helped raise hundreds of thousands of dollars for the prevention and treatment of birth defects.

And, as with all my endeavors, this work is dedicated to my best friend and soul mate, Buddy, who has absorbed, questioned and challenged my newspaper articles, children's books and short stories for fifty-five years, encouraging me to strive for excellence.

Contents

*"It has been the providence of Nature to give
this creature nine lives instead of one."*
The Greedy and Ambitious Cat. Fable Bidpai.

Prologue

I DO NOT KNOW IF HUMANS are reincarnated. During my twenty-five hundred years of coming and going I have met a few who appeared to have "old souls" but, because they cannot remember anything about their past lives, it is impossible to be sure. Cats, on the other hand, possess an immaterial entity that categorizes our past existences with exact details.

Some cats have new souls. They're the ones who live in the streets and howl on top of fences. We old-timers can spot them a mile away. Then there are those who have been around several hundred years. They're smart enough to wrangle their way into human houses where they stuff their stomachs and disappear. They spend their entire lives begging from door to door. These neighborhood cats are clever enough to coerce their meal tickets into believing they belong to them. They rub against their legs with their furry bodies and allow themselves to be petted but they have no loyalty. Many of the houses own dogs. Those poor loyal ignoramuses spend their entire lives following their owners around, sitting up on command, begging for attention and remaining unconditionally faithful until death, determined to have their love returned. And what is their reward? Their humans are flattered that some scraggly cat finds its way to the doorstep to scarf down their food. It doesn't take a psychoanalyst to know why dogs hate cats.

Those of us who have been here since ancient times are far more sophisticated. Two thousand five hundred years ago, the Egyptians revered cats as sacred. They even had a cat goddess named Bastet that protected their homes against disease and evil spirits. If you look closely at my profile you will see the nose and mouth of Bakmuk, the favorite Royal Daughter of the Great Pharaoh Ramses II.

"I believe cats to be spirits come to earth.
A cat, I am sure, could walk on a cloud without coming through."
— Jules Verne

The Bird

I HAVE SPENT THE PAST EIGHTEEN years with a twenty-first century family that appears to be aware of my spirituality if not my past existences. I believe this has been my best life of all and I am saddened to have it come to an end.

Two weeks ago I crawled into the closet attached to the master bathroom to begin my dying process. If I were a wild cat I would find refuge in an isolated cave that would protect me from predators but, having been domesticated for several thousand years, the closet satisfies my primal instincts. I am not in pain. I do not feel anything. During the past six months, I have lost fourteen of my previously voluptuous twenty-two pounds. My doctor describes my condition as acute kidney failure and gives me intravenous fluids but no encouragement.

There's a baby mocking bird outside the large picture window over the Jacuzzi tub. It flaps its wings and whacks itself against the glass as if to break through and enter the house. Of all things, a bird has come to take me away from this life, and a mocking bird at that. How prophetic! The bodacious bird has appeared at the window every morning, chirping and staining the glass with its excrement. The first time the human I call *mom* saw it she smiled and said, "Good morning little bird. Don't bang against the window like that. You'll hurt yourself." After a few days she looks from the bird to me more closely. A troubled look comes over her face as she grasps the incredulous possibility of its determination. Without true comprehension, she turns to the window and confronts it with a muffled cry. "Go away. Sakie's not ready to go with you." She forces my lips apart with two fingers and shoves an antibiotic down my throat. I'm too weak to bite or spit the horrible tasting pill across the room.

How does she know? How can a human understand? I try to tell her I am ready. I no longer care about eating. Even when I think I'm hungry I cannot bring myself to taste anything. She brings my favorite canned and dry foods. They smell good but I have no appetite. She continues to bring them anyway, gently coaxing. She even tries to stimulate my senses with tuna that I never refuse. I am genuinely sorry and truly appreciate her efforts. I try to tell her this with my eyes but most images except the little bird have become cloudy. She picks me up and cradles me in her arms, kissing each of my pink ears and then the top of my white head as she has done for almost eighteen years. She is going to miss me.

I would like to say that I will miss her also but it's not true. You see, I've been through this four times before, although the past three are the only ones I recall.

I open my eyes and see a small dish being placed under my nose. I raise my head to the ambrosial aroma. Shrimp! These are not regular shrimp but rock shrimp like they advertise in fancy restaurants. She has split, buttered, broiled and chopped them so fine that I do not have to use my old decayed teeth to chew. I lick the sauce. I gum the delicacy and try to let it slide down my throat. Perhaps it will give me enough strength to share my story.

Sakie's Rock Shrimp
Yield: Approximately 4 servings

24 rock shrimp

¼ pound unsalted butter

2 tablespoons olive oil

1 clove garlic, minced

2 tablespoons fresh lime juice

1 teaspoon minced tarragon leaves

1 tablespoon minced parsley

1. Turn the broiler to high and position the rack directly underneath the heat.
2. With a very sharp scissors or kitchen shears, cut open the clear inside shell of the shrimp to expose the meat. Remove the dark vein. Place the shrimp, meat side up, in a shallow pan.
3. Combine the butter, oil and garlic in a saucepan and bring to the bubbling point. Add the lime juice.
4. Pour over the shrimp. Broil 2-3 minutes only, basting one time in-between. Do not overcook. The rock shrimp are very tender and cook faster than regular shrimp.
5. Toss with the tarragon.
6. Remove the shrimp to 4 plates. Spoon the sauce over. Sprinkle with parsley.

"It is man's sympathy with all creatures that first makes him truly a man. Until he extends his circle of compassion to all living things, man will not himself find peace."
— Dr. Albert Schweitzer

The Beginning

SUSAN FOUND ME UNDER A bush on her way home from school. I was approximately three weeks old, a tiny white ball of fur not much larger than her sixteen year-old hand. My sister was there also but our mother was nowhere to be found. I fear that she has met with ill fate from one of the fast moving cars I can see from our hiding place.

She called to her friend a few steps behind. "Laura, I've found kittens". Laura reached down and cuddled my sister. Susan scooped me into her arms. They carried us to her car. The ride seemed endless and my whole body was shaking. Where was I? Nothing was familiar. There had been no automobiles in my former life. The teenagers looked odd also. What strange clothing they were wearing, and their long hair was loose around their shoulders instead of neatly braided or tied up.

"What shall we name them?"

"I'm going to call mine Sushi because I'm hooked on it."

"Do you think my Mom will be angry if I call this one Sake?"

"You mean like the hot wine at the Sushi place? Why would she be angry?"

"Because she might think I've been drinking."

Susan thought for a minute. "If I spell it *S-a-k-i-e*, she won't figure it out."

They giggled and Susan held me closer.

Susan dropped Laura off and continued to drive until we

crossed over a small bridge that connected to an island. She parked in front of a brick house with a pillared front porch that held up a balcony I remembered as neo-classical they now called "Georgian".

The minute we entered the house I saw the dog. He was the size of a large German shepherd with a huge coat of white fur. His head was shaped like a golden retriever's and was larger than my entire body, but he had tulip ears like a collie, one of which folded perfectly from its pointed crest and the other that drooped rather listlessly over his forehead. Susan set me on the floor next to him and said, "Sakie, this is Sam. We found him on the highway when he was only six months old. He had a neck injury from a collar that was too tight and a broken tooth from biting through his chain when he escaped from a truck."

We recognized each other immediately. He was Bodger, the white dog of the Ojibway Indians, now known as the Chippewa. We had been soul mates since the 1600s during my third life. I was called Tao then. We traveled together, sent by the Spirits to test hospitality and bring good fortune to all who made us welcome. I sat on the shore of frozen streams in Minnesota while he bravely swam through the ice into the current to catch walleye bass for our supper. He became the immortal of the Indian legend when he staggered into the Ojibway camp hungry and bleeding from his encounter with a bear cub he tried to befriend. I was at his side, licking his wounds. The old Indian woman saved his life by healing him with an ointment made from the marsh plant, commonly known as cattails. She brought us into the warmth of her home and fed us wild rice, the healthy staple of the tribe. She knew the white dog and the white cat that traveled together were an omen of good luck. We would bring fortune to the entire tribe because she took us into her care. That was the night the two of us became immortal as a team. Now finally, after living my fourth life alone and lonely, we were once again united by a twist of fate in the form of a teenage girl in a modern world. He lay down on his side with his legs outstretched. I crept into the long white hair of his chest and fell asleep.

Sam's Walleye Bass with Caper Sauce
Yield: Approximately 6 servings

Equipment: Fish poacher or deep skillet with cover
6-7 pound whole bass, cleaned, head on or off, skin left intact
Salt and freshly ground black pepper to sprinkle
2 cups dry white wine
2 cups water
1 tablespoon minced fresh dill or 1½ teaspoons dried dill

Juice of 1 large lime
2-inch piece ginger, peeled and sliced thin
1 onion
Leaves and top cut from whole stalk celery
1 clove garlic, split
¼ teaspoon Dijon mustard
Optional: 1 pound large shrimp (U26-30)

1. Have the fishmonger clean and scale the fish, slitting it open from the head to the tail along the belly.
2. Sprinkle inside and out lightly with salt and pepper.
3. Set the fish into the poacher (skillet). Combine remaining ingredients, stirring well, and pour over the bass. Bring to a boil. Cover with the top tilted to allow steam to escape. Boil 2 minutes over high heat. Reduce heat to medium-low. Ladle broth over. Cover tightly and steam 7 minutes longer. Ladle broth over again. Cover and steam about 6 minutes longer, or until fish flakes with a fork and there is no sign

of pink or opaque within. Do not overcook. Cooking time should be approximately 15 minutes total.

4. Remove fish from poacher to a large platter.
5. Carefully remove the skin from the top of the fish with a sharp knife. It should slide off easily.
6. For a glorious feast, add one pound peeled and deveined (tails on), large (26-30) shrimp to the broth and bring to a boil. Cook 1 minute only. Remove with a slotted spoon and arrange over the top of the fish.
7. Strain the broth into a saucepan to use as the base for Caper Sauce.

Caper Sauce
Yield: Approximately 2 ½ cups or more

2 tablespoons unsalted butter
2 tablespoons all-purpose flour
2 ½ cups strained broth from the poached fish

¼ cup heavy cream
½ cup tiny capers
¼ cup chopped fresh dill
Salt and pepper to taste

1. Melt unsalted butter in a saucepan over low heat. Stir in flour. Slowly stir in broth, cooking until mixture thickens slightly and becomes smooth. Stir in cream. Mixture will continue to thicken. Do not allow it to boil. Stir in capers and chopped dill. Pour ½ cup over the fish and serve remaining sauce on the side. Decorate with tiny red tomatoes for color.

Chippewa Rice for Sam and Sakie
Yield: 4-6 servings

6 ounce package wild rice (not instant)

6 ounces large white mushrooms, sliced thin

4 tablespoons butter

1 medium onion, chopped into small pieces (not minced)

2 ribs celery, chopped into small pieces (not minced)

½ cup yellow or orange bell pepper, chopped into small pieces (not minced)

1 teaspoon salt

1 teaspoon pepper

3 cups water

Optional: 12 toasted chestnuts in season

1. Wash the rice in a strainer under cold running water.
2. Rinse the mushroom caps quickly under cool water. Do not soak. Cut off the bottom of the stems. Slice thin.
3. Melt the butter in a saucepan. Sauté the onion, celery and pepper over low heat until they are limp but not colored.
4. Add water and bring to a boil. Stir in rice, salt and pepper. Bring all to a boil, stirring. Cover. Reduce heat to low and cook 50 minutes, stirring often. Set pot into the bottom of the double boiler, which has been filled one-third with hot water. Leave in its water bath over very low heat until ready to serve.
5. Score each chestnut with a cross on its flat end. Place on foil or a baking sheet in a 350°F oven for 15 minutes or until the skins pop open. Remove the skins and chop the nuts coarsely. Stir into the rice directly before serving.

Minnesota Wild Rice and Mushroom Soup
Yield: Approximately 8-10 cups

The dried Porcini mushroom creates a very rich soup. For lighter fare, choose Crimini or exchange dried for fresh Portobello mushrooms. Remove the brown or black gills from the inside of the Portobello before slicing and cooking.

½ cup wild rice from Minnesota

3 cups boiling water

2 ½ quarts beef broth (or 6-10 ounce cans Campbell's® Beef Broth Bouillon)

½ cup dried mushrooms (Italian porcini or crimini)

2 sweet onions, chopped fine

Optional: 1 clove minced garlic

2 tablespoons butter or butter substitute

Salt and pepper to taste

1 pound fresh white mushrooms, sliced thin

Touch of cayenne, if desired

⅓ cup fat-free half and half

1. Pour 2 cups of the boiling water over the rice and allow it to stand 2 hours. Drain and cover with remaining 1 cup boiling water. Bring to a boil. Reduce heat to medium, cover and cook until tender (approximately 50 minutes).
2. Stir in the beef broth.
3. Soak the dried mushrooms in hot water to cover for 2-3 minutes. Drain and chop the mushrooms fine. If Portobello mushrooms are exchanged, remove the dark gills, chop, and set aside.
4. Sauté the onions with the dried mushrooms (and garlic) in the butter until soft in a small pan. Stir into the soup. Bring to a boil. Reduce heat to very low. Cover and cook 30 minutes or longer. Taste for salt and pepper. Add a touch

of cayenne, if desired. Remove from the heat until ready to serve.

5. To serve: Add the white mushrooms, stir in half and half, and bring to just below the boiling point.
Steps 1-4 can be made a day in advance.

"The smallest feline is a masterpiece."
— Leonardo da Vinci

I Discover
Who I Am

WHEN THE FAMILY CAME HOME, they agreed I
was the prettiest kitten they had ever seen. They set food down
for Sam and a small dish of canned kitten food for me. I was
so famished I swallowed it in one gulp. At the end of the day
Sam followed her parents into their room and Susan carried me
through hers into a bathroom where I was dropped into a box
filled with kitty litter.

"Now this is where you go when you have to go."

I already know this. After all, I am a cat or will be in
a few short months when I am no longer a kitten. Cats are
instinctively clean. We don't have to be told where to go and
what to do.

I lay my head on the carpet next to her desk while she does
her homework. She closes her books and carries me to her bed
and tucks me into the fold of the blanket. Then she crawls under
the covers, turns off the light and, lightly scratching the top of
my head, curls onto her side and falls asleep.

Her shoulder length chestnut brown hair covers the pillow,
cascading in all directions. Golden highlights mixed with deep
burnished auburn catch the moonlight that shines through the
window, beckoning me to crawl within. The sensation of that
hair is the most wonderful experience of any life I have known.
Its soft warmth envelops my entire being. I work my way farther
into the luxuriant waves and fall into a euphoric deep sleep. It is
to become my sanctuary, my secret place for the next year. Even

after she abandons me for another I will dream of nestling in that pasture of loveliness.

When I wake in the morning, I quietly jump to the floor so as not to disturb her. As I pass the door to the bathroom, I see another kitten. I stop, turn, and move slowly toward it. The kitten is white just like me. I cock my head to the left. It cocks its head at the same time in the same direction. I raise my paw to touch it and it raises its paw at the same time. Instead of feeling the soft pads of another kitten, my paw collides with something hard. I jump back and let out a meow. Its mouth is open in the shape of a meow also but the only sound is coming from me. I walk back and forth in a circle watching in puzzlement as it does the same. I fall onto my stomach with my legs stretched out and wait for what seems an endless length of time. At long last Susan comes through the door. She sits on the floor next to me. I see a girl who looks exactly like her sitting next to my kitten. I meow in puzzlement again.

"Sakie, do you see the pretty kitten in the mirror? It's you. That's Sakie in the mirror. You are the prettiest kitten of all"

Mirror? Me? I remembered seeing my reflection in the stream near the walls of the Gotokuji Temple outside Tokyo, Japan. It was in the early 1700s. The Temple had been built several years earlier in 1697. I looked exactly like the paintings of the Bobtails on the walls. The water reflected my large oval, slanted eyes and high cheekbones. Most important was the break in my whiskers, which matched the perfect "pompom" tail that distinguished us as the revered breed of nobility. I knew the Japanese had once considered Bobtails to be good luck symbols but we no longer lived with the wealthy or in the Emperor's Palace. In 1602 we were turned out to the streets and farms to rid the country of the mice known as vermin that were eating the cocoons of the silkworms. Without silk, Japan would become an impoverished nation. Even the most revered "kink-tail" Bobtails were let free to fetch for themselves. It seemed that good fortune for the ruling class was the silkworm rather than the Bobtail. My discovery that I embodied the perfect characteristics of the white long-haired Bobtail, complete with scattered patches of black and red on my gleaming coat and dwarfed bushy tail, saddened me. The beautiful Bobtail cat that was brought to Japan by the Emperor, Ichijo, in the tenth century to be pampered and sheltered was now banished to oblivion. I had all the credentials of royalty, but I was born at the wrong time. This was my fourth life, approximately eighty years after I had traveled with Bodger. I lived it alone, lonely and hungry. We beautiful Bobtails were never meant to be hunters. In 1693, the German naturalist, Englebert Kaempfer, went to Japan and, after studying my breed, wrote "They have no mind to hunt rats and mice but just want to be carried about and stroked by women".

I ponder if who we are and the time capsule in which we are created is an accident of birth or planned by some inventor fixated in a mood of diabolic or gratuitous humor.

I gaze at the kitten sitting next to Susan. The bright rays of the morning sun with their miniscule particles of left-over dancing stardust reflect through eyes as green as the sea on a clear summer's day. I am no longer a Bobtail. My white hair is beginning to grow thick but my tail is too long and exceptionally wide. There were neither black nor red patches in my fur and my features are beginning to resemble those of the Egyptian profile of the Royal Princess, Baknuk, one of the sixty daughters of Pharaoh Ramses II. Suddenly I remember. I was the royal cat of the princess. It must have been my second life. This was the era when we were valued for our mysterious qualities and idolized as bearers of good fortune.

"Thou art the Great Cat, the avenger of the Gods, and the judge of words, and the president of the sovereign chiefs and the governor of the holy Circle; thou art indeed...the Great Cat."
— Inscription on the Royal Tombs at Thebes

I Am an Egyptian Mau

I REMEMBER MY LIFE AS THE royal cat of the beautiful princess Bakmut as though I were living it today. She was the beloved daughter of Ramses II, the greatest king of ancient Egypt and Nefertari, his favorite queen. Historic records tell us that he took almost two hundred other wives, who produced a total of ninety royal sons and sixty daughters during his lifetime because of his desire to create a strong society bearing his royal blood.

The Egyptians of the 19th Dynasty believed cats were daughters of their gods, Osiris and Isis. Osiris was the god of rebirth and Isis was the goddess of the sun and the moon. It was believed that the glow from cats' eyes captured the setting sun and held the light during the darkest time of the night so the Egyptians could remain safe until the light of day appeared again. The goddess of beauty, motherhood and fertility possessed the head of a cat and the body of a woman. Her name was Bastet and she was revered as one of Egypt's most important deities.

Everything in the kingdom belonged to Pharaoh including all the cats. He had decreed that cats of any color could not be harmed unless by a verdict passed down by the high priests. It was against the law to injure or kill a cat and, if anyone did so even by accident, the punishment could be death.

Bakmut, as all Egyptians, regarded cats as demigods. Cats were not given names then. They were called 'mau' or 'miu', or 'myeo', which means "to see" in Egyptian. It was also the sound they made. The Egyptian Mau is the only naturally spotted domestic breed of cat and is also the oldest domesticated cat in history tracing its ancestry back 4,000 years.

I was presented to the Princess a few months before her twelfth birthday. Bakmut had a porcelain complexion with King Ramses' sea-green eyes and golden hair that shimmered with red highlights. She also possessed a kind disposition, strong moral character and an unusual intellectual and spiritual capacity for deciphering the problems of both the physical and metaphysical worlds for someone who had not yet reached maturity.

The Pharaoh himself carried me to her in his gigantic hand that consumed my entire little kitten body. My fur was pale silver with the beginnings of random black spots in what would become a dense and resilient coat of medium length. My tiny ears stood erect showing off the delicate, almost transparent shell pink inside. My legs and tail had the exquisite pattern of black bars or bracelets and my silver-white neck gave the impression of a wide broken necklace. My almond shaped eyes were a pale translucent green delicately outlined in black like the cosmetically enhanced eyes of the Egyptian women who painted the design to connect with the spiritual powers of the goddess Bastet. Every detail of my face and body promised to become an exquisite Mau.

The princess bowed to her father's presence, keeping one alert eye fixed on me.

"My Princess", said Ramses, "I have brought you a Mau to bestow good luck and fortune. You must cherish and care for her as you would a goddess. You must protect and love her and she will reward you in return."

He placed me in her arms. My voice made a soft meow as

I cuddled against her delicate skin. I looked at her luxuriant golden red hair and knew I had found a home.

Every morning her hand maidens bathed her in goat's milk and rubbed her flawless porcelain complexion with a lotion made from the purest honey in Egypt. I was given a cup of the same milk in a golden bowl to ensure the growth of shining fur. Then they dressed her in fine linens and tied up her waist length hair. Fresh flowers were inserted into the last loops of the braid before the loose hair at the end was weighted down with a golden clip. Bakmut then adorned her wrists with golden bracelets and her neck with turquoise, placing lighter ones around my neck to match her own. When the grooming ritual was finished, we paraded through the palace for everyone to admire the lovely preteen and her precious kitten.

During the next year she changed from a child into a great beauty, and I from a shy kitten into an elegant full-grown Mau. I now walked beside her with graceful cheetah-like stride that showed my well-developed muscular strength. I absolutely adored her. I lived for her attention and, when she spoke to me, I chortled a soft melody of connected meows to show my joy. She would look into my eyes, understand my thoughts and know I was expressing my devotion to her.

At barely fourteen years of age she was not only breathtaking to behold but had reached a development of maturity most humans did not possess until their youth was gone. It was rumored throughout the Palace that she was being groomed to marry her handsome eighteen year-old half-brother, Nakhti, that meant "strong", whom Ramses seemed to be favoring as his successor. She, like Nefertari, would be the confidant and advisor to the next great Pharaoh as his Consort. She would also be the sole decision maker in his absence when he was with his armies or in the desert overseeing the building of Temples to the gods.

Nakhti came to visit us in our royal apartment several times each week with a banquet prepared by a master chef and served with great aplomb by slaves in honor of his courtship. Because most Egyptians were primarily vegetarians, sumptuous salads of seitan, chickpeas and feta cheese followed by fava beans marinated with pomegranate, anise and cumin were artistically arranged on gold and bronze plates.

Although he had a handsome face and enchanting personality, there was something about him I did not like. At first I thought I might simply be jealous of her attention to him but my instincts said I should watch him carefully. There was something that bothered the Princess also. Perhaps it was that he didn't seem really interested in her as a person, but only in her birthright. She wanted to know all about him, from his favorite foods to his mission in life. He seemed completely disinterested in anything other than her beauty and position as Ramses' favorite daughter. Ramses and Nefertari had instilled within her their religious convictions that necessitated daily worship of the gods and a passion for preservation of the temples, colossal statues and obelisks in the new capital in Upper Egypt known as Pi-Ramses. When she attempted to share her father's dedication to the gods of Egypt, Nakhti changed the subject. Was it that he wasn't religious or was she not considered intelligent enough to carry on a conversation of any practical importance? She even tried to share her knowledge that her father's best friend, Moses the Hebrew, was in charge of building the city that would live for eternity, but Nakhti paid no attention. He always seemed distracted as though his thoughts were elsewhere when she spoke.

One afternoon, while she was engrossed with mystical

music on her harp, I sneaked out of the royal apartment. Moving quickly through the immense hallways of the palace I worked my way to the opposite side where Pharaoh's many sons lived. Each had his own apartment similar to those built for the royal daughters. I went from one to another but could not locate Nakhti. As I walked on I saw two young men, whom I knew to be his half-brothers from different mothers. One of these was Akhom. His name meant *"Eagle"*, which suited his strong body and keenness of eye perfectly. He was studying to be an architect with expectations of fulfilling his dream to spend his life in the desert building shrines to the glory of the gods. Although he was without ambition to become the next Pharaoh, I thought he should consider the position because he was my favorite of the many sons I knew. He also visited my beloved Bakmut but, rather than courting her as a potential fiancé, he spent the entire time describing his designs for a mammoth statue of her father that would include his loyal lion and dog sitting at his feet. Although he spoke only of his architectural inspirations, his adoration of her was obvious even to a cat. But she, who usually was so bubbly and effervescent, said nothing in return. Sometimes he would bring gifts of fresh fish from the Nile that he had caught and cooked himself, and delectable dates pounded with nuts and honey that were molded into small treats. He came without his slaves, offering only himself in hopes she would fall in love with him as he had with her. When she gave no encouragement of his efforts, he returned quietly to his quarters. As soon as he reached the garden and could no longer see her, she tiptoed to the window and followed him with her eyes until he was out of sight.

Akhom was sitting by his window playing the lyre and humming. When he saw me, he set the instrument down, making sure the fragile strings were protected. I jumped onto his lap. Scratching the top of my head, he said, "You are a welcome visitor. Tell me what you are doing here."

I mewed that I was searching for his half-brother, Nakhti. He looked directly into my eyes and, with the wisdom of the great eagle, understood everything. He pointed to the east.

"You'll find him three apartments straight ahead. I wish you hadn't come. You are not going to like what you find. And, since I can confide in you, I sure wish you could talk so you could tell the Princess how much I love her."

I rubbed up against him in appreciation.

"I'm sorry little Mau, but the King has chosen him, not me. Our Princess deserves nothing less than to be Queen so I will not even try to win her. But I am distressed about his choice. She deserves better than a perfect face and winning personality that mask an imperfect character."

I jumped down and moved east in the direction where he had pointed. When I found the apartment I entered. In the distance I could hear people speaking. I moved toward the sound. There stood the unhappiest sight of my young life. Ramses' first choice of successor to the throne and intended groom to my beloved was kissing princess Kepi. Her name meant 'Tempest' in Egyptian and I could see it suited her. Kepi was the daughter of one of Ramses' less important wives. I had seen that wife on several occasions. She was ambitious and rude. As Nakhti held Kepi in his arms I heard the last words of his sentence….

"….and, when I become Pharaoh, I will marry you and not Bakmut. You will become my Queen. The King will be dead. He will never know. It is you and only you that I love. Bakmut would threaten my power as Pharaoh as soon as she gained insight into my intentions to replace Ramses' statues with those of me as Egypt's true god."

I turned and ran all the way back to Bakmut, who did not even notice I had been gone because she was still playing her harp and humming. I called out to the Great Cat Goddess, Bastet, for help.

Oh dear sister Bastet, daughter of sun god Ra, protector of women, children and domestic cats with the Eye of Ra that sees all, raise your sacred rattle, Sistrum, over my darling Bakmut and shield her from evil. Dearest beloved goddess of pleasure, music and dancing, bring her joy with the spiritual and gifted Akhom. I promise to revere you and celebrate your power on your feast day each October 31st.

The next afternoon the Great Pharaoh, Ramses, called for Bakmut to come to his quarters at exactly two o'clock. Her maidens dressed her in her finest linen and set an elaborate wig on her head. She was immediately transformed from a princess into a young queen.

Ramses and Nefertari greeted her warmly, giving her many compliments with regard to her maturity and beauty. Several minutes later prince Nakhti arrived magnificently attired in starched white linen embroidered with gold threads. Shiny gold necklaces were tied around his neck and bracelets adorned his arms. He wore a headdress of ostrich plumes and his sandals were tied with golden strings. He bowed deeply to the King and Queen and then to Bakmut. He was indeed a magnificent specimen of assured young royalty. I looked at my princess and her despicable groom and made the most serious blunder of my life. I hissed. I actually hissed at him, curling my refined lips around my perfect white teeth. And then I heard a low growl. At first I didn't know where it came from. Then, as all eyes focused on me, I knew. I would surely be in disgrace. I might even be taken away from the Princess. A Royal Mau never showed displeasure or temper. A Royal Mau never interrupted the Great Pharaoh. I had committed an unforgivable act and deserved to be punished.

Ramses, who understood the thoughts and emotions of all creatures, simply stared at me as Bakmut grabbed me into her arms.

"My Father", she apologized, "I have never seen Mau act like this before. Please forgive her. I promise she will never do this again."

Nefertari whispered something into Ramses' ear. He turned to his courier and commanded,

"Send for Prince Akhom immediately."

Several minutes later Akhom was ushered into the group. He bowed to Pharaoh and stepped backward waiting for the reason he had been summoned. When I saw my young Prince not properly dressed for the occasion and breathless from running to fulfill Pharaoh's dictate that had interrupted his studies, I committed the second blunder of my life. I broke free of Bakmut's arms and jumped up to his chest, clinging to his shoulders. I did not mew or chortle in my usual soft melodious voice, but let out a low howl that sounded like a death chant. He was so embarrassed that his ears reddened with his cheeks. The Great Pharaoh reddened also. But, before he could reply to the actions of an imprudent cat, the conniving Princess Kepi burst into the room. She approached Ramses without bothering to bow, shocking everyone in the royal group.

"You cannot make Nakhti marry Bakmut. He's mine. He loves me and only me. He promised that I would be his Queen, not her."

Bakmut let out a gasp. She was suddenly aware that her

half- brother had planned to betray her. I dug my claws into my Prince's shoulder and mewed that this was the moment to make his move. *It's now or never,* I told him. He let out a little sound of pain as a smattering of blood trickled from the wound. And then, holding me securely in his arms, he walked over to Bakmut. As he handed me to her, he whispered,

"Mau is smarter than all of us. She knows we were meant for each other and she's not afraid to say so. I do not care if I'm not Pharaoh. I just thought you deserved to be Queen. If you're not going to be Queen, I want you to be my wife."

Bakmut wrapped her arms around his neck and sank her head in his chest with me in-between getting quite squashed.

"Is this true", asked Pharaoh, "would you give up being Queen to marry Akhom?"*

"Yes, Father."

Ramses conferred with Nefertari and announced, "I decree that my beloved daughter will be given in marriage to my Royal son, Akhom."

This was the greatest hour of all my lives.

Prince Nakhti's Courtship Seitan Salad
Yield: Approximately 4-6 servings

Egyptian wild lettuce was eaten as an aphrodisiac. Arugula and watercress are a modern version with Romaine. Tofu or tempeh can be substituted for the seitan for gluten intolerance. Seitan is a versatile food. The recipe below can be served over rice with heated garbanzos, tomatoes, and red onions. Seitan can also be sliced into pieces and grilled or fried.

For the seitan:

6 ounce package seitan mix (Health food stores and on-line)
¾ cup water

1 tablespoon Italian seasoning
1 tablespoon garlic salt

1. Mix the seitan mix with the water in a mixing bowl. Stir with a spoon until mixture holds together. More water may be needed. With floured hands, knead to form soft elastic dough.
2. Shape into a rectangle 5 inches long X 1½ inch deep. Cut the rectangle lengthwise into 6 even pieces, approximately 3" long, 1 ½" high, 1" deep. If the ends are rounded, form to match the center slices.
3. Fill a 2 quart pot with water. Add the Italian seasoning and garlic salt. Bring to a boil. Drop the seitan into the water. Return the water to a boil. Stir to make sure seitan are not sticking to the bottom. The seitan will then rise to the top. Cover. Reduce heat to low. Boil gently 45 minutes or longer, until the seitan is very tender.
4. Remove seitan to a bowl. Strain the liquid over. Leave in the liquid until ready to use. Refrigerate if storing overnight.

Make Your Own Seitan

Vital wheat gluten and nutritional yeast can be found on-line or in health food stores. There are many brands from which to choose.

1 cup vital wheat gluten (high protein wheat flour)
¼ cup nutritional (deactivated) yeast
1 teaspoon grated fresh ginger or ½ teaspoon ginger powder
1 tablespoon grated fresh garlic or 1 teaspoon garlic powder
6 cups water or vegetable broth for the cooking process
1 tablespoon tamari sauce

1. Combine wheat gluten, yeast, ginger and garlic. Stir in 1 cup of the broth and the tamari sauce, adding more broth as necessary until the dough forms. Knead the dough by hand (not machine) until it is elastic. Shape into 2 loaves.
2. Pour remaining broth into a pot. Bring to a boil over medium heat. Add the loaves. Reduce heat to low and simmer 30-45 minutes, or until the seitan is firm. Remove from the heat and cool to room temperature in the broth.
3. Follow above instructions for the recipe with seitan mix.

Preparation of Finished Seitan

¼ cup lemon juice
½ cup Italian extra-virgin
  olive oil
½ teaspoon garlic salt

Freshly ground black pepper
Commercial Thai sweet chilli
  sauce (actually spicy)

To Serve:
1. Remove the seitan from the bowl and roll into several large pieces. Slice into 3rds to create rectangles.
2. Whisk together the lemon juice, oil, garlic, and salt.
3. Coat the bottom of a non-stick pan with the Thai chilli sauce.
4. Over high heat, sear the seitan rectangles on both sides. Or brush with the sauce and set over a gas grill to sear.
5. Toss the lettuce with some of the dressing. Arrange the salad items on separate plates. Drizzle a bit of the dressing over the vegetables. Set the grilled seitan on top.

For the Salad:
Arugula, watercress, and Romaine lettuce, broken into small pieces,
Kalamata or another Middle Eastern flavored olive, pitted.
Red onion, sliced very thin on the round
Cucumber, sliced very thin on the round
Optional: Cubed Feta cheese
Optional: Garbanzo beans (chickpeas)
Beefsteak tomatoes, seeded and cut into cubes

Prince Nakhti's Fava
Yield: 4 servings

15-20 ounces canned fava
beans, drained
2 cloves garlic, minced with
a knife
1 small sweet onion, minced
1 English cucumber (seedless
long variety)
¼ cup pomegranate seeds
2 tablespoons finely minced
scallion greens
¼ cup finely minced parsley
leaves

1 tablespoon lime juice
1 tablespoon white balsamic
or champagne vinegar
⅓ cup extra virgin olive oil
½ teaspoon or more to taste
ground cumin
1 teaspoon ground coriander
¼ teaspoon ground anise seed
Salt to taste
Fresh black peppercorns to
grind over all

1. Drain the beans and combine with remaining ingredients
   in a bowl.
2. Refrigerate several hours or overnight.
   Serve over a lettuce leaf with pita bread on the side. Or fill
   pita bread pockets.

The Eagle's Fresh Catch
Fish of the Nile
Yield: 4 servings

4 tilapia fillets
¼ teaspoon salt
2 tablespoons unsalted butter
1 teaspoon flour
½ teaspoon turmeric
1 cup concentrated chicken
   broth

1 small fennel bulb, julienne
   into fine strips
⅓ cup heavy cream
1 tablespoon chopped fresh
   tarragon or 1 teaspoon
   dried

1. Sprinkle the fillets with salt. Melt the butter in a skillet. Sauté quickly on both sides until golden brown but not overcooked. Remove the fillets from the pan to a warm platter.
2. Over low heat in the same skillet that the fish was cooked, stir in the flour. Add turmeric. Add the chicken broth, a little at a time, stirring. Add the fennel strips and continue to cook until the sauce has thickened. Stir in the heavy cream.
3. Stir in the tarragon. Spoon the sauce over the fillets and serve immediately.
   Note: Tarragon must be added at the end. Tarragon that cooks too long can become bitter.

Delectable Dates
Tiger Nut Sweets
Yield: Approximately 24 balls

8 ounces pitted dates
1 tablespoon cinnamon
¼ teaspoon nutmeg
2 tablespoons honey

2 tablespoons cool water
½ cup ground blanched
   almonds

1. Slice the dates and place into a food processor. Add cinnamon, nutmeg, and honey. Process until slightly chunky. Add water. Process again until mixture holds together and is very gooey.
2. Rinse hands in cool water and shake off excess. Shape into marble size balls by rolling in the palms of your hands.
3. Rinse and dry hands.
4. Roll in ground almonds and remove to a serving plate. Do not cover the plate.
   These delectable treats can be made up to a month in advance and stored in an airtight container. Stack in layers separated by wax or parchment paper.

"Thousands of years ago, cats were worshipped as gods. Cats have never forgotten this."
— Anonymous

Christopher

S<small>USAN'S OLDER SISTER</small>, M<small>EGAN</small>, <small>CALLED</small> to say
she was bringing her six week-old baby to stay with us. *Mom*
and *dad* were ecstatic. Their firstborn was coming home with
her firstborn. The house buzzed with excitement. A miniature
crib, known as a *barcelonnette* in French because it was on
rockers to lull the infant to sleep, was set up in the guest room.
The wood sides and cupola hood were covered with lace and
blue bows. Around the inside of the crib was what they called
'bumpers' to cushion Christopher and keep his little legs from
touching the hard wood surface. It was covered in the same
lace as the sides and cupola. The sheet that covered the mattress
had darling paintings of puppies and kittens. At the end of the
mattress was a tiny blue blanket with white puffy embroidery
of a puppy dog. It was a *barcelonnette* fit for a Prince.

The first words out of Megan's mouth are, "And, keep that
cat out of Christopher's room. I don't want a cat near my baby."
As soon as she leaves, I tiptoe into his room.

My beautiful Egyptian Princess, Baknuk, was fifteen
years old when her first child was born. She was the perfect
mother from the minute her baby arrived. The crib was exactly
21.888 inches long, the measurement of the Egyptian sacred
cubit. Standing next to the crib was the statue of Anket, the
goddess of fertility, wearing her tall headdress made of ostrich
feathers. In one hand was a scepter, her symbol of authority,
and in the other an Ankh, the symbol of life. As soon as

Christopher

Baknuk's baby was placed in his crib she picked me up, set me at his feet and chanted, *Bring this child good fortune. Bring joy and health and power to my first-born.* I knew my duty. I lay absolutely still while she brought another smaller Ankh to the crib and placed it across my front legs that I had stretched out in anticipation. Every Egyptian knew that this cross with a loop on top provided magical protection to all who revered its presence. I remained absolutely still without moving a muscle for thirteen minutes for the ancient ritual where the number thirteen brought immortality. At the exact second thirteen minutes ended she carried me to the garden and fed me fresh fish from the River Nile as my reward. We repeated this every day for the next thirteen days. There has never been a cat as proud as I.

I look at Christopher sleeping in his crib. He is as beautiful and perfect as the Egyptian baby I recalled. I leap upward onto the sheet decorated with puppies and kittens. There is not enough room in the miniature crib for me to stretch out so I gently curl my body into a ball at his feet. I can see the Ankh between us in my memory and begin to count. When I contemplate thirteen minutes, I smooth the sheet, jump down to the floor, and stroll contentedly to the kitchen where I feast on kibbles I imagine are the fish of the Nile. I repeat this pattern every day as soon as Megan leaves the house.

On the twelfth day I am so pleased with myself that I do not visit Christopher until late in the afternoon. I am in his crib exactly eleven minutes when I see the shadow of a figure coming through the door. Has Megan returned early or am I so remiss that I did not gauge the time correctly? She takes one look at me, points a finger, and screams,

"Cat, get out!"

I cannot move.

"Cat, Get out!"
I cannot move.
"Mom", she shrieks, "Get that cat out of my baby's bed".
Mom is in the kitchen and does not hear the commotion.
Sam enters the room with a low growl.

> *Sakie, get out of the crib.*
> *I have 45 seconds left,* I said.
> *Sakie, get out, NOW!*
> *I have 35 seconds left.*

Megan: "MOM, where ARE you?"

> *Sakie, get out.*
> *I have 15 seconds left.*
> *Sakie, this is not the 12th century B.C. and you are*
> *not in Egypt. Get out of Christopher's crib.*
> *I have 5 seconds left.*

Megan: "CAT, GET OUT!!"

> *3-2-1. Bye, little Christopher. See you tomorrow.*

Sam pushes me out of the room and Megan places the palm of her hand on Christopher's chest to make sure her baby is breathing. When we are out of hearing distance, Sam snarls,

> *What is your problem?*
> *He's so precious. I have to protect him.*
> *This is crazy. He is already protected. This is a*
> *different era. You are upsetting the family.*

Just one more day, Sam, please? Tomorrow will mark the thirteenth day.

Do you mean you are planning to spend thirteen minutes in that baby's crib again tomorrow? It's Saturday and Megan will not be at work. How do you expect to spend thirteen minutes in that crib without her finding out?

I don't know. But I have to complete the magic. Please Sam, help me.

I'm sorry, Sakie. I cannot. They trust me.

That's the whole problem. They always trust a dog but not a cat. Why don't they trust a cat?

Because cats are unpredictable and imprudent.

We are not! I'm predictable and prudent.

You call jumping into the crib with a newborn human baby predictable and prudent?

It is for me. I don't understand the big fuss. By the way, what does 'prudent' mean?

It means the ability to make responsible decisions. It means 'trustworthy'. Cats have a reputation for unexpected behavior that lacks good judgment and self-restraint. Humans are nervous around cats. There's an old superstition that goes all the way back to sixteen hundred when people swore that cats put their noses into sleeping babies mouths and sucked their breath away. Even in our modern times a cat in the house has sometimes been blamed when a baby actually died from the inexplicable sudden infant death syndrome known as SIDS. It's a good thing you're not black or you would really be in trouble. You must remember the witch hunts in England where black cats were thought to be evil bearers of

*bad luck. Halloween night is still a dangerous time
for the black cat.*
*I would never suck away my baby's breath. My duty
is to bring him good fortune.*
They do not know this.
Please Sam, help me. I have to complete the magic.
*I give up. I'll help you but only because I remember
that you accompanied me to the Ojibway Indian
camp on that night long ago. I will go with you
tomorrow, but never again will I be a part of your
mischief.*

Early the next morning, as soon as Megan goes outside to swim laps in the pool, Sam motions for me and we sneak into Christopher's room. Without wasting any time, I jump into the crib and curl into a ball by his precious little feet while Sam stands guard at the door whining softly. Refusing to let him aggravate me, I concentrate on my task at hand. Suddenly I remember.

*Sam, can you find some Sntr to scatter around the
crib?*
What are you meowing about?
*Sntr is the hieroglyphic word for divine fragrance
or incense. It means that which makes divine. Look
at him. Isn't he just divine?*
*Sakie, get on with it. You're running out of time. If
we're caught, we'll both be back on the road Sntring
for more than incense!*

Exactly thirteen minutes later, my mission completed, I jump out of the crib and the two of us stroll leisurely into the kitchen where *mom* is busy preparing her version of Niçoise Salad from fresh tuna. As soon as she sees the white dog and the white cat she fills a bowl for us. We happily share this modern feast from the Nile.

Sakie's Reward
Niçoise Salad
Yield: Approximately 4 servings

The Dressing

3 tablespoons tarragon
  vinegar (or more to taste)
½ cup olive oil
1 clove garlic, crushed
1 teaspoon Dijon mustard

½ cup scallion greens,
  chopped
Salt to taste
Freshly ground black pepper
  to taste

1. Combine ingredients and refrigerate.
    Note: Tarragon vinegar can be homemade from apple cider vinegar and fresh or dried tarragon leaves. Insert the leaves into the bottle to infuse at least 24 hours before using.

The Salad

1 pound fresh tuna fillet
  (salmon may be exchanged)
Salt and pepper

1 teaspoon fresh lemon juice
Extra virgin olive oil

1. Season the fillet on both sides with a sprinkling of salt and black pepper.
2. Brush well with the lemon juice.

3. Cover the bottom of a non-stick skillet with extra virgin olive oil.
4. Heat over medium until bubbles form.
5. Cook the fish on one side no longer than 3 minutes.
6. Turn and cook, covered, until no signs of pink or opaque color remain within. Do not overcook. Remove from the pan and set aside.

PUT IT TOGETHER

Romaine lettuce, chopped (Arugula may be added, leaving leaves whole)
1 pound cold red bliss potatoes, skins on, boiled until just tender and sliced thin
12 cherry or grape tomatoes
8 or more Kalamata or Niçoise olives
Handful of large caper berries
2 hard-boiled eggs, shelled and quartered
1 English seedless cucumber, peeled and sliced thin
Fresh tarragon leaves to garnish
Optional: white Italian cannellini or white northern beans, anchovies
Optional: Chopped Feta cheese

1. Chop the lettuce and combine it with the arugula. Toss with some of the dressing.
2. Divide onto 4 plates.
3. Divide the tuna (salmon) into 4 pieces and set on top of the lettuce. Surround with remaining ingredients to serve with extra dressing on the side.

*"For every house is incomplete without him,
and a blessing is lacking in the spirit."*
— Christopher Smart, <u>Jubilate Agno</u>,
on his cat, Jeoffry, 1763

Time Out

Aʟᴛʜᴏᴜɢʜ I ᴍɪssᴇᴅ ᴍʏ ᴍᴀᴍᴀ and sister, I was having a splendid time in my new life. Sam let me sleep against his warm furry stomach as often as I pleased. Because we were exactly the same color and our hair was so long, we blended into one. The huge white dog was an ideal hiding place for a tiny white kitten. Even after I had grown to maturity, we continued to nap together every evening until he was called into the master bedroom and I into Susan's.

At first I thought her parents were really weird. When they spoke to me it was as though they were also my parents. "Be a good girl, Sakie, and *mom* will give you a treat. Look Sakie, *dad* and Sam are home from work." I knew the names of my owners in Egypt and Japan but did not consider them my *mom* or *dad*. I was a cat. The only name I had in Egypt was Mau, which meant Cat. Even when beautifully pampered and revered I was still a cat. My mama was a cat, not a human. I never knew my dad but no cat ever has. Cats only have mamas, even if breeders know who our dads are. And our mamas leave us to be on our own as soon as we are able to fend for ourselves. It's unheard of for a grown cat to be taken care of by her mama. Yet, humans in this strange new world speak to their adopted dogs and cats as they do to their children, referring to themselves as *mom* and *dad* when we do not look or act like them at all. Unnatural as it seemed at the time, it was also comforting and I felt very secure in a way I had not known in any of my previous lives.

There were marvelous places in this house to explore. It was not the Egyptian palace I remembered but it was large and comfortable with ample rooms to entertain me.

I had been there approximately three weeks when I found the scratching wall. I started at the bottom digging my razor sharp young claws into the surface. It took several weeks to work my way all the way to the end. When this was accomplished I began to explore upward. I crawled all the way to the top securing my feet with my claws in the same manner an experienced mountain climber uses his ice axe. Up, up, up I climbed, creating perfectly raveled patterns of hanging strings as I went. Suddenly my proud achievement came to an abrupt halt. *Mom* was running toward me shouting in time with wildly flailing arms. "Stop, Stop", she screamed. "Get down from my grass-cloth wallpaper!" She pulled me off the wall by the back of my neck the way my mama used to carry me. My hind legs immediately dangled in mid-air while my forepaws hung immobile and my eyes crossed slightly into a glazed stare. Mama cats instinctively know there is a nerve behind the ears of her babies' necks that temporarily paralyzes them. She gently pinches this nerve with her teeth to carry us without a struggle. How this human mama knew the technique would remain a mystery. Her voice was sharp. "No! No! No! You've ruined my most expensive grass-cloth wallpaper! Bad! Bad! Sakie Cat is a Bad Girl!" Then she carried me into Susan's bathroom and shut the door, leaving me with my dish of water and box of kitty litter. This was what the family called "time out" or punishment inflicted upon very young children. I later learned from my beloved Susan that "time out" is called "grounded" at the teenage level of development. It was to mark the beginning of many "time-outs" for my young misdoings.

Other than time-out periods this new world was absolutely

perfect. I slept in Susan's luxuriant hair all night and basked in the warmth of the sun that flooded the screened-in back porch in the morning. I also discovered the kitchen. It was the best room in the entire house and where I would spend the majority of my life for the next eighteen years.

There was no place in any of my lives I had dedicated to fine cuisine that compared to *mom's* kitchen. There was always something wonderful happening. *Mom* wrote a newspaper column about food. She was also writing a cookbook. And she had dinner parties at least once a week. She spent hours in the kitchen experimenting and creating new recipes. There were banana trees bent to the ground with dwarf Cavendish bananas by the water and a mango tree that shaded the front yard. At the end of June, when it became really hot, the mangos ripened into a glorious mixture of red and deep yellow exuding a scent that permeated the neighborhood as an aphrodisiac. She made mango chutney from those that were still slightly green, saving the ripe ones for mango bread combined with tiny Key limes, their skins perfectly ripened into soft yellow. One entire shelf of the freezer was filled with peeled and sliced mangos to create sauces off-season. We were all convinced that it must have been a mango tree in the Garden of Eden because anyone could have an apple, but a juicy ripe mango was something to die for.

The family's favorite cuisine was fresh seafood of all descriptions that would have made a dozen cats covet my good fortune.

The aroma of fresh Yellowtail snapper dipped in Betty Crocker® Potato Buds and browned in butter brought a soft gurgle from within my chest. The sound of a hammer cracking our native stone crabs produced a series of uncontrollable meows. Fresh Florida spiny lobster tails boiling in a pot of water sharpened my senses, particularly when being prepared for a soup called Bisque. But it was shrimp that made me lose all semblance of conscience. With one leap I was on the kitchen counter bathing in their tantalizing perfume.

"Down, Sakie", *mom* said in a stern voice, but I could see she was smiling. "You'll get yours, I promise".

First she removed the shells from the cooked shrimp. Then with a small sharp knife she cut down their backs to expose the dark veins, which she removed under cool, running water. Next she gently pulled off the overlaying flaps of sumptuous throw-a-way. These she methodically placed into a small bowl. When they were all clean, she cut up the reserved flaps and presented them to me as the perfect hostess would present a gourmet feast to Royalty.

"My lady", *mom* declared ceremoniously and set the plate on the floor. Then, standing very straight, she moved her right arm in an arc to her right, and with her left arm in front of her, folded her left leg slightly in back so her toes barely touched the floor, which caused her right knee to bend in a bow. "Bon appétit, mon petit chat!"

This is my best life of all. I am finished with vermin forever. I have moved on.

Banana Bread

Yield: 3 - 8X3 inch loaves or 2 - 8X8" square
pans or 5- 3 X 6 X 2 inch mini loaves

1 teaspoon baking soda
2 teaspoons double acting
  baking powder
⅛ teaspoon salt
2 cups sifted all-purpose flour
½ pound butter, softened to
  room temperature
2 cups granulated sugar

4 jumbo eggs, room
  temperature
1 tablespoon vanilla extract
¼ teaspoon almond extract
½ cup sour cream
2 cups puréed ripe bananas
  (approximately 4)

1. Preheat oven to 350°F.
2. Sift together the soda, baking powder, salt and flour.
3. Beat butter, adding sugar slowly on low speed. Turn speed to high and beat until white and fluffy. Turn beaters off occasionally to scrape the sides and bottom with a rubber spatula.
4. Add eggs, one at a time, on medium speed until well-blended, scraping the sides of the bowl after each addition. Beat 3 minutes longer.
5. Add vanilla and almond extracts.
6. Add sour cream on low speed. Mixture may appear to curdle. This will disappear in the baking.
7. Purée bananas in a blender and beat in immediately.
8. Add flour mixture on low speed. Turn off beaters. Scrape bowl. Beat again on medium speed for a few seconds, or until flour is incorporated. Do not over-beat. Over-beating will toughen any cake.

9. Fill the pans. Set the rack one-third from the bottom of the oven and bake as follows:
    8" loaves: 40-45 minutes
    Mini loaves: 30-35 minutes
    8X8 inch pan: 30-35 minutes
    8 inch cake pans: 30 minutes
    Test for doneness by inserting a wood pick in the center. When it comes out "clean" with bits of cake fragments sticking to it, your bread is done.
    Note: Ripe mango or peach purée can be substituted for the bananas. Exchange orange extract or a tablespoon of orange juice for the almond listed above.

Mango-Lime Bread
(2 loaves)

3 ½ cups all-purpose sifted flour
2 teaspoons baking powder
1 teaspoon baking soda
¼ teaspoon salt
1 tablespoon cinnamon
¼ teaspoon nutmeg
Optional: 1 cup chopped pecans or walnuts
4 jumbo eggs

1 ½ cup granulated sugar
1 cup canola oil (or another vegetable oil of choice)
½ cup chopped mangoes
¼ cup Key lime juice
2 tablespoons mango or peach liqueur
1 cup ripe mangos
1 cup ripe peaches

1. Preheat oven to 350°F.
2. Sift the flour, baking powder, baking soda, salt, cinnamon and nutmeg together. Add the nuts and set aside.

3. Beat the eggs. Add the sugar, oil, chopped mangoes, lime juice, and liqueur.
4. Stir the flour into the batter.
5. Fill 2 greased bread loaf pans. This is not necessary if pans are disposable aluminum
6. Bake 30-35 minutes, or longer, until a wooden pick comes out clean with a bit of the dry dough still sticking to it.
7. Slice and serve topped with chopped fresh mangoes.
Note: These freeze beautifully.
This bread is a lovely accompaniment to luncheon chicken or tuna salad or as a breakfast starter for the day. Fresh peaches in season may be substituted, or the two fabulous fruits can be joined together

Garden of Eden Chutney
Yield: Approximately 2 quarts

10 pounds mangos, half green, half at firm-ripe stage (Approximately 8 mangos)
3 large onions
2 large green bell peppers
2 large red bell peppers
3 tablespoons minced or crushed garlic
2 limes
8 ounces crystallized ginger

10 tamarind pods
3 cinnamon sticks
1 tablespoon salt
2 teaspoons ground allspice
¼ teaspoon cayenne pepper
4 cups golden raisins
4 cups dark brown sugar
3 cups light brown sugar
1 cup apple cider vinegar
2 cups toasted pine nuts
12-one pint jars

1. Pick or buy a combination of green and ripe mangos. Wash, peel and dice the mangos into cubes. Place into a large soup pot.

2. Chop onions and green peppers into small cubes by hand. If you use a food processor, keep the onions chunky. Do the same with the bell peppers. Mince the garlic. Add all to mangoes in soup pot.

3. Soak the ginger in warm water 10 minutes, or until softened. Remove the hard shell and root strings from the tamarind and soak with the ginger. Chop ginger and add to pot. Remove the soft pulp covering the pods and add to the pot.

4. Add cinnamon, salt, allspice, cayenne, raisins, sugars and vinegar.

5. Bring mixture to a boil, stirring often. Reduce heat to medium and boil gently one hour, stirring often. Taste. If too tart, add more brown sugar to taste. Cook another half hour.

6. Toast pine nuts lightly. Stir into chutney. Fill Mason jars while still hot and seal according to directions.

   Serve with fish, lamb, duck, pork or chicken. This is marvelous over ice cream.

   Note: Chutney improves as the flavors marry. Its shelf life will be between 10-12 months.

Sakie's Snapper
Yield: 2 servings

2 snapper fillets, weight 6-7 ounces each

Salt and pepper to sprinkle

½ cup instant Betty Crocker® Potato Buds

2 tablespoons extra virgin olive oil

1 tablespoon unsalted butter

2 tablespoons Pinot Grigio wine

1. Pat the fillets dry with paper toweling. Sprinkle with salt and pepper. Dip into the potato flakes to coat on all sides.
2. Heat the oil in a non-stick shallow pan.
3. Place the fish, skin side down to brown.
4. Add the butter. Turn the fish and brown on the flesh side.
5. Add the wine. Turn the fish. Bring to a quick bubbly boil. Remove fish immediately to warm plates. Serve over Pineapple-Mango Relish.

Mango-Pineapple Relish
Recipe may be doubled and tripled
Make several hours in advance for flavors to combine
Yield: Approximately 1 cup

1 small yellow or orange bell pepper

½ cup ripe pineapple, cubed

1 ripe but firm mango

1 tablespoon minced fresh cilantro leaves

1 tablespoon minced scallion greens

Pinch of cayenne pepper

Pinch of white pepper

1. Slice the pepper in half and remove the seeds. Slice 6 thin strips from the pepper to reserve for decoration.
2. Place the pepper halves on a piece of disposable foil skin side up under the broiler close to the heat. Broil until black. Immediately close the foil tightly over the pepper. Wait 10 minutes. The skin will peel away easily. Cube into tiny pieces with a knife.
3. Remove the skin and core of the pineapple. Cube into tiny pieces with a knife. Mix with the pepper. Peel the mango and cube into small pieces with a knife. Carefully mix into the pepper and mango.
4. Fold in minced cilantro leaves, scallion greens, cayenne, and white pepper.
5. Refrigerate several hours. Remove from the refrigerator 30 minutes before serving. Divide on to the center of 2 plates. Set the fish fillets on top. Decorate with reserved pepper strips and cilantro leaves.

Sakie's Stone Crab Salad
Yield: 6 servings

2 cups cooked stone crab meat, cut into chunky bite-size pieces

1 cup mayonnaise or more to taste

½ teaspoon salt

⅛ teaspoon black pepper

2 teaspoons lemon juice

½ teaspoon Dijon mustard

1 tablespoon white horseradish

2 celery ribs, chopped

2 tablespoons chopped cilantro leaves

Baby lettuce greens, grape tomatoes, flavored olives or a selection of fruit in season

1. Crack the stone crab claws and remove the meat. Cut into chunky bite-size pieces.
2. Combine mayonnaise, salt, pepper, lemon juice, mustard, horseradish and celery. Carefully fold in crab meat.
3. Set the baby lettuce onto 6 plates. Scoop the crab salad in the center. Sprinkle chopped cilantro over the tops. Decorate the outer edge of the plates with grape tomatoes and olives or a selection of fruit.

Sakie's Shrimp with Rémoulade Sauce
Yield: 4-6 servings 1st course

1 pound small shrimp (41-50   Water to cover
   per pound)

Rémoulade Sauce
Yield: Approximately 1 cup

1 cup mayonnaise   ½ teaspoon Dijon mustard
2 tablespoons chili sauce   ½ teaspoon (or more) dill
1 heaping teaspoon white   Chopped iceberg lettuce
   horseradish

1. Cover shrimp with water in a large pot. Bring to a boil. (Watch carefully or water will foam over the top creating a mess to clean up) Reduce heat to medium and boil 1 minute. Remove from fire and let stand 5 minutes. Pour off water and rinse shrimp in cold water. Peel and devein immediately. (Or, purchase shrimp cooked and cleaned.

If shrimp are frozen, pour boiling water over them for a fresher flavor) Refrigerate in a bowl.

2. Make **Rémoulade Sauce**: Combine mayonnaise, chili sauce, horseradish, mustard and dill in a bowl and stir until smooth. (Add more horseradish to your taste) Toss well with the shrimp and serve over chopped lettuce.

Note: Sauce recipe may be doubled to serve on the side.

*".....if I am shaven, then my strength will leave me and
I shall become weak, and be like any other man."*
— Holy Bible, New King James Version, Judges, Chapter 16."

A cat's claws are like the hair of Samson's head.
— Sake 1986."

My Operation

SUSAN FOUND A RED RIBBON left over from a Christmas present in her closet. It was bright and shiny and she and her friends swished it over my head watching me try to grab it with my paws. I jumped. They laughed. There was also an extra ball of yarn in mom's knitting bag. They held the big ball and teased me with the long piece of yarn hanging from it until I finally grabbed the whole ball, shaking the yarn loose until my paws and head were all caught in the soft strands. This made them laugh again. They bought a ball with a bell in it and I chased it all over the house. They bought a larger ball that I could roll with around the room. Then I was presented with a tiny red and yellow soft chicken that made a tinkling sound when I pushed it. Someone brought a soft gray mouse and someone else came to the house bearing a tiny elephant and another ball. By the time I was six months old my "toys" were strewn all over.

Sam gave me a stern look.

You have too many possessions. You are a spoiled cat. I have one tennis ball that everyone throws for me to fetch. You should play with the family and not a bunch of toys. I will give you thirty minutes to choose your favorite thing. The rest have to go.

I gathered everything and piled it into the center of the room to take inventory. I guessed I didn't really need three balls. The ribbon had become frayed and shabby from so much tugging. Besides, I knew Susan would find another newer ribbon for me to play with. The yarn was mom's so Sam couldn't take that from me. He knew she did not need his permission to pull it out of her bag. That left the mouse, the elephant and the chicken. I really loved the chicken best and figured he would not count the number of balls. So I quickly covered the yarn and the chicken and the smallest ball with my furry body.

> *I said only one toy.*
> *But the yarn belongs to mom, and I want the ball.*
> *Then the chicken goes.*
> *Please, Sam, don't take my chicken. I sleep with my chicken every night. It's my very favorite.*
> *Make up your mind. I'm losing patience. And, don't think I'm stupid. I know Susan will find another piece of ribbon and mom will let you tangle up in her yarn.*
> *O.K. O.K. Take the ball. I'm tired of it anyway.*

Over the next week I watched from the window while Sam methodically removed my toys one at a time, carrying them in his mouth outside to the garden where he buried each of my possessions in a different place around the bushes. Since I was not allowed outside he knew I couldn't retrieve them.

I soon grew bored with my chicken and decided to explore for hidden treasures. Then I saw something under the table. It was a perfect circle about the size of a five cent piece but it was so clear it was translucent. I could see through it like a window. I tapped it with my paw. It flipped into the air. I tapped it again and it flipped higher. I flipped it all over the room. Then I picked it up between my teeth. I swallowed. Oops! It slid down my throat and was gone.

For some reason I wasn't hungry when the family served dinner and for the first time in my life refused to eat. I felt something uncomfortable floating around my breast bone. It didn't hurt. It was just a strange sensation. I refused breakfast the next morning and dinner the next night. In the morning they took me to the doctor who x-rayed my whole body. There in the photograph of the inside of my tummy was my lovely round toy. But it wasn't a toy. It was a transparent plastic disc that separated glass from a wood table top for it to "float" rather than lie directly on the wood where moisture can gather. It had somehow gotten loose and fallen to the floor. Now it was floating in my tummy without any hope of coming up or going down because it had no weight to enable it to move or be moved. It would float there forever unless it was surgically removed.

The last thing I heard our veterinarian say before the anesthesia put me to sleep was something about de-clawing so I could no longer destroy the wallpaper and furniture. "We do it all the time to indoor cats". And then there was blackness.

When I awakened there were stitches and bandages everywhere. My tummy didn't hurt but my paws were in massive pain. What had happened to me? Where were my perfect, cherished, sharp claws? I licked at the stitches for two weeks and whimpered. *Mom* held me in her arms and cried. How could she have allowed them to do this to her precious cat? In the following weeks my front paws healed but I continued to shake them in the air expecting the nails to pop out from inside. The back paws were so sensitive for six months that I wouldn't let anyone touch them. Eventually the pain subsided. I became so accustomed to my new paws that I could not remember ever having claws. But during that time of convalescence I had learned a new method of defense. My tiny razor-sharp teeth sent a stronger message than claws. When people got on my nerves I let them know it. If they petted me for too long a time on my head or scratched my back too close to my tail or entered my "space" where I was napping, I opened my mouth and hit them hard with the point of my sharpest upper tooth, which humans refer to as the "eye tooth". It always punctured their skin and left a deep purple hole. If they really annoyed me, I hit them with my whole mouth of teeth. These maneuvers were always directed at adults, never children, unless the child in question was purposefully trying to 'kill the cat'. Aside from these occasional outbursts I remained my loving, loyal, charming self, devoted to my family and their friends. But whenever the subject of de-clawing arose, the family became adamant about removing only the front claws so we might have the back claws for protection if we wander outside the house. I wasn't going anywhere. I knew better.

"After dark all cats are leopards"
— Zuni Proverb

Growing Up

I HAVE GROWN UP. I AM now a full-fledged respectable cat, and a perfectly gorgeous one at that! My long coat is pure white without a hair of another color anywhere. My eyes are an iridescent light green and my perky little soft pink ears match my tiny pointed nose. My profile is disturbingly human, resembling the Egyptian Royal Princesses of three thousand years ago, and my stance is of finely-bred aristocracy. When I sit erect with my head up and my front legs perfectly straight so close together that they almost touch without leaning on each other for balance, no one doubts my pedigree. No one asks. It is taken for granted that I am a pure bred Angora – or something.

I have also begun to assert my authority in the house. No Palmetto bug, known to most as the huge American cockroach indigenous to Florida, escapes my scrutiny. These ugly beasts might be smart and fast but I'm smarter and faster. The trick is not to let them see or hear me coming or they will disappear into a crevice before I can blink one eye. I tiptoe up behind them and tap the nerve behind their necks with the tip of my paw. This immobilizes them long enough for me to flatten them with one whack. I would never squash them or eat them. This would be contrary to my dignity. I just walk away and leave them to eventually be found by a member of the family who removes them to the garbage with Kleenex or paper toweling.

Then there are the little lizards. We have zillions of them outside in the garden. They eat the small insects and bugs, including baby roaches, so they're good to have around. These green and brown little reptiles are native to Florida. The proper name for them is Anoles, but most people refer to them as Chameleons because they can change color when threatened. These little pre-historic leftovers would never come into a human's house on purpose but they're not very intelligent and do not know where they are going most of the time. They do not know how to hide like the Palmetto bug and they are not nearly as fast. Instead of ducking into a dark crevice, they scurry up a door or wall and lie absolutely still, theorizing that I cannot see them in their colorless camouflage. I lie still also, pretending to be asleep, and I wait. When they think the coast is clear, they move slowly down. When they reach the floor, I pounce. The trick is to get the whole body in my mouth at once. If I only get the tail, it snaps off and the little fellow escapes, leaving the severed piece still wiggling. So, I attack from the front, letting the tail hang out of my mouth. If the family catches me in the act, they get all upset and try to pry open my jaws. I would have dropped the creature eventually, stomped on it and walked away, but they leave me no alternative. I swallow it whole. I would wager that I have several dozen Anoles somewhere in my stomach.

I can also sing. The first time I realized I had a voice was shortly before Christmas. The rich aroma of fruitcake from candied cherries, pineapple, apricots, crystallized ginger and raisins that had been marinating in rum for three days was ready to be removed from the oven. *Mom* inserted a long wood skewer into its center and was pleased to see it came out dry with bits of cake attached. It was absolutely perfect. She set it on the counter to cool, raised the oven temperature from 275°F to 350°F, and placed a large ham glazed with sweet and savory seasonings on the bottom rack.

Combining ingredients into a bowl for Christmas cookies, she began to sing. Something about the pitch made me sit up very straight.

Silent night, Holy night.

When she got to the verse, *Sleep in heaavenly pee-eee-ce*, her voice went way up, holding on to *pee-eee-ce*. I couldn't help myself. A sound emerged from deep in my throat that was the same high note right on key with hers. *Sleep in heaavenly eeowoooo....* She looked at me in wonderment.

"Sakie, that was marvelous. Let's do it again."

Sleep in heaavenly pee-eee-ce. When she reached the high note, I raised my chin and joined her. *Eeowoooo....* White flour began to fly everywhere as she clapped her hands in admiration.

Bourbon Ham
Yield: 10-12 servings

9-10 pound bone-in shank half cooked ham ("tenderized")
½ cup Kentucky bourbon
6 whole cloves
½ cup orange juice
¼ cup pineapple juice from the canned rounds below
1 cup Coca Cola®, ginger ale or ginger beer

¼ cup brown mustard (Gulden's®)
¾ cup dark brown sugar
1 teaspoon Angostura Bitters®
20-ounce can sliced pineapple rounds
Orange slices

1. Cut excess fat from the ham. Combine the bourbon, orange and pineapple juices, Coca Cola® (or ginger ale), mustard, sugar and bitters and rub them into the ham. Insert the cloves equally around. Refrigerate several hours, or overnight.
2. Transfer the ham to a shallow roasting pan and bake in a preheated 350°F oven one hour, basting frequently. Place the pineapple rings on top with a cherry in the center of each. Baste. Bake 15 minutes longer.
3. Remove to a serving platter. Slice oranges on the round with their skin and place on the platter. Spoon the gravy over.

High Note Peppermint Cookies
Yield: Approximately 40 cookies

1 cup butter, softened
½ cup granulated sugar
2 jumbo egg yolks
1 tablespoon vanilla extract

2 ½ cups all-purpose, sifted flour
2 cups finely-chopped candy canes
Colored sugar, green or red

1. Preheat oven to 350°F.
2. Cream butter and sugar until white and fluffy, scraping sides of bowl several times.
3. Add egg yolks on medium speed. Scrape sides. Beat again.
4. Add vanilla.
5. Beat in flour on low speed until smooth, scraping sides several times. Fold in chopped candy canes by hand.
6. Roll dough into 1-inch balls. Flatten with the palm of your hand. Place on a non-stick cookie sheet.
7. Bake 14-16 minutes or until firm to the touch.

Sakie Sings Sugar Cookies
Yield: Approximately 60 cookies

2 ½ cups all-purpose flour
1 teaspoon baking powder
¼ teaspoon salt
Optional: ¼ teaspoon nutmeg
½ pound butter, softened

1 full cup granulated sugar
1 tablespoon vanilla
2 jumbo eggs, beaten
Red and green colored sugar
for Christmas

1. Sift together the flour, baking powder, salt (and nutmeg). Set aside.
2. Beat the butter and sugar together until white and fluffy on high speed of a hand held mixer. Add the vanilla and continue beating until incorporated. Beat the eggs with a fork in a small bowl and add. Beat until incorporated.
3. Beat in the flour, a little at a time.
4. Form the dough into 2 balls and refrigerate, wrapped in wax paper, several hours.
5. Preheat oven to 350°F.
6. Roll out 1 ball ¼ inch thick on a floured surface. Cut out cookies with a Christmas cutter or by pressing a drinking glass or small empty can upside down to create circles.
7. Sprinkle the cookies lavishly with colored sugar.
8. Bake 9-10 minutes until golden.

Mom's White Fruitcake

Yield: 8-9 inch round tube pan or 3 disposable
aluminum pans 8 X 4 X 2 ½

8 ounces candied red cherries
8 ounces candied green
cherries
8 ounces candied pineapple
6 ounces dried apricots
4 ounces sugar glazed
(crystallized) ginger, diced
8 ounces golden raisins or
dried cranberries
2 cups dark rum
2 ½ cups sifted all-purpose
flour (If you use cake flour,
sift 3X before measuring)
1 tablespoon double acting
baking powder
½ teaspoon salt
1 cup (½ pound) butter

2 cups granulated sugar
6 jumbo or 7 extra large eggs
¼ cup orange juice
1 tablespoon vanilla extract
8 ounces blanched, slivered
almonds
8-9" tube or Bundt pan, or 3
disposable aluminum loaf
pans to wrap as gifts
Mixture of liqueurs: ¼ cup
brandy, ¼ cup Gr. Marnier,
¼ cup Frangelico or
Amaretto
Cherries soaked in cream
sherry to decorate the top
after 4 weeks.

1. Cut cherries, pineapple and apricots into irregular bite size pieces. Dice the ginger fine. Leave the raisins and cranberries whole. Stir in the rum to marinate 24-36 hours. Turn over several times to saturate evenly.
2. Preheat oven to 350°F.
3. Combine flour with the baking powder and salt. (Cake flour mixture sift 3X)
4. Cream butter and sugar on high speed of an electric mixer until white and fluffy, scraping bowl often.

5. Add eggs, one at a time, on medium speed. Beat 5 minutes or longer. Scrape sides and bottom of bowl. Add orange juice and vanilla.
6. Add flour on low speed, scraping sides and bottom several times.
   Remove the batter to a large bowl. Stir in the marinated fruit and almonds. (Note: The fruit and rum sink to the bottom. Before filling the pan(s), turn the mixture over several times with a large spoon to incorporate them evenly.)
7. Grease the tube pan by rubbing the bottom, sides, and center tube with vegetable oil. Spoon the cake mixture in loosely, patting it smooth on top. Disposable pans do not require greasing.
8. Place the cake(s) on a rack set ⅓ from the bottom of the oven. Reduce oven temperature immediately to 275°F. Bake the cake 2½ hours, or until a wooden skewer inserted comes out dry. If cakes are baked in aluminum disposable pans, timing will change to 1½ hours.
9. Line a round container or Christmas tin with cheesecloth and invert the cake. This is not necessary when baked in disposable pans.
10. Combine the brandy with the Grand Marnier and Frangelico. Brush the cake(s) heavily. Cover tightly. Let the cakes age 3-4 weeks, basting each week with the same combined liqueurs.

*'When rats infest the Palace a lame cat is
better than the swiftest horse"*
— Chinese Proverb

Blackie Saves
Siena

LOUNGING BY THE POOL ONE Sunday, *mom* and *dad* were preoccupied with neighbors who had dropped by. Sam was sleeping in the sun and I, as usual, was bored. I decided to sneak away to find what might be of interest beyond the bushes at the edge of our property.

I had just pushed the leaves aside and taken a few steps into the darkness when I detected something breathing. Not one to be easily frightened, I meowed, *Is something here?*

Something big and black appeared in front of me. I mean something very big and black with a huge amount of fluffy fur that resembled a baby bear. Although I was unable to sit on my hind legs to offer him my signature Bobtail greeting because of all the foliage, I said most politely, *I'm Sakie.*

> *Pleased to make your acquaintance. They call me 'Blackie'.*

I curbed the impulse to make a snide remark about the originality of his name and instead said, d*o you have a home in the neighborhood?*

> *Oh yes, I have the most luxurious home. In fact, it is my very first home ever. Not many black cats have had homes throughout history. Humans believed we were the bearers of bad luck. We were not even allowed to*

cross anyone's path for fear of being killed. It was only because I led the army that saved the city of Siena, Italy, from total extinction from the bubonic plague that I was born again in this life to be rewarded.

I contemplated this preposterous statement for a moment. *Do you really believe that what we did in our last life determines our reward or punishment in our next one?*

Absolutely. What other reason would there be to do good?

I wanted to say that, although I've always been good, I was not rewarded in two of my lives. Well, actually, maybe only one was terrible. I would never have exchanged my life on the road with Sam for any home with humans. Instead I said, *tell me how you saved Siena.*

Cats were originally brought to Rome by travelers from Egypt. At first everyone liked us because we got rid of the rodents. But, then, they became frightened that we had some sort of evil magical powers and accused anyone who had cats of witchcraft. They killed as many cats as possible and, when they did, the rat population exploded. Then, in 1348, the terrible Bubonic Plague came to Siena. The 'Black Death', as it was called, killed fifty million Europeans and would quickly kill over eighty thousand in Siena, which was most of our population. Everyone believed it was the cats that spread the disease and they systematically murdered every last one they could catch. Black cats were singled out first as witches who turned themselves into black cats to roam the streets and spread the plague. The few of us that once called this beautiful city our home had to run for our lives. I saved myself by hiding in the underground springs where hundreds of rats were also living. Attached to these rats were thousands of fleas that had reached Italy by ship from China. One day I watched the fleas biting the rats and realized that they were the cause of the disease. Some of the rats died but they multiplied so quickly new ones took their place. Then, the fleas made their way to homes and humans were infected. And, then, humans infected other humans because the deadly bacterial disease was airborne. The only solution would be to kill all the rats before everyone in Siena died. And the only ones who could accomplish this would be the cats. I knew at that moment that I had to save mankind.

I sneaked into alleys and the crevices of buildings where they were hiding. I recruited them, one by one, to enlist in the cause. Although terribly frightened, every cat, toms and felines alike, accepted the challenge until we had an army of several hundred. With me in the lead, we marched through the city to every place inhabited by the rats and slaughtered them all. When the people of Siena realized what we had done, I was proclaimed a national hero. They invited us into their homes to share their food and wine. There was a special lady by the name of Paola Danti from Florence who made Tuscan Crostini from beef and chicken livers and served it hot on little toasted bread rounds. She was the only one in Siena who knew the recipe and, although others attempted to copy, it never tasted the same. We formed perfect lines in front of her doorstep where she gave each of us our reward for saving her children from the disease.

Linguine alla Vongole was one of my favorite choices that every Italian mamma made for her family. I was also invited into a home where tiny carpet shell clams brought to Siena from the Mediterranean Sea were prepared with pasta in iron pots set over a blazing fire on the hearth. The aroma of fresh garlic and extra virgin olive oil squeezed from Tuscan olives was more than any cat could hope for. However, as much as I loved seafood, my very favorite dinner was Coniglio con Funghi Cremini.

I had to interrupt. *Con-who with what,* I asked?

Sorry, my little non-cosmopolitan. Coniglio con Funghi Cremini is an incredible meal of fresh rabbit and mushrooms. Most Americans have never eaten rabbit. They think it is Bugs Bunny or an Easter present for children. Italians eat more rabbit than chicken and prepare it in as many ways as you do your chicken. When we prepare our chicken, it is always embellished with a sauce or combined with other flavorful ingredients. We find your roasted, broiled and even fried chicken quite boring. Tell your humans to look up a Tuscan favorite called Vitello di Tonnato, which means Veal with Tuna. It's more economical made with chicken and just as good. Now, if you will allow, I will conclude with the best part of my place in Siena's history.

71

One night a little after two o'clock in the morning when the survivors of the plague were asleep, the Vicar of Siena beckoned me to his chambers. Before he spoke, he set a small cup on the floor in front of me. In it was soft warm custard infused with Marsala wine that had been carried by friends seven hundred miles all the way from Sicily. When my tongue reached the bottom, it became covered with a thick powder of sweet fresh chestnuts from the neighboring city of Lucchesi. As I mewed in appreciation, he confided his greatest fear.

"Blackie", he said, "For centuries, our beautiful city of Siena and the lands south to Montepulciano and north to Florence have been renowned for wine and food, as well as artists whose paintings combined our Byzantine heritage with Christian humanism brought forth by the Franciscans and Dominicans. The Black Death killed so many people that there are not enough workers to plant or harvest the Sangiovese grape that produces our Chianti and Brunello wines. If we do not repopulate our city, we will lose our livelihood and our culture and become prey to being conquered by the armies from Florence. I do not know what to do or where to turn for help."

I ran to the bell tower and grabbed the rope with my claws. It began to swing and, as I was carried back and forth, the bells rang out so loudly they awakened everyone in the city. Nine months later, hundreds of babies were born. I did this at exactly two o'clock every morning for the next year until every home was filled with new life.

*And that, my dear new friend, is the story of how
I saved Siena.*

I was truly overwhelmed but thought it time to return to
my family before I was missed.

I enjoyed meeting you. I hope to see you again, I said, and
backed out of the bushes just in time to see Sam looking for me.
I thought it best not to share Blackie's story with him because
he probably would not believe it.

Paola Danti's Crostini for Blackie
(Pat di Toscana)
Yield: 16 toasts

1 clove garlic, minced
1 medium onion, minced
1 tablespoon minced capers
4 anchovy fillets
½ cup extra virgin Italian
 olive oil
¾ pound lean ground sirloin
¾ pound chicken livers,
 trimmed
½ teaspoon dried sage, or 1
 teaspoon minced fresh leaves

½ teaspoon salt
¼ teaspoon black pepper
2 tablespoons Chianti wine
1 teaspoon tomato paste
 mixed with ⅓ cup water
½ cup strong beef broth
16 thin slices Italian bread
 (If large, cut into halves),
 toasted on 1 side only

1. Combine the garlic, onion, capers, and anchovies in a food
 processor. Mince fine.
2. Heat the olive oil in a skillet. Add the mixture from the food
 processor. Add the ground beef and cook, stirring constantly
 until meat is cooked. Add livers and cook until just done, but

still soft. (Overcooked livers become bitter) Add sage, salt and pepper. Remove from heat and put into a food processor with a steel blade. Turn on/off a few times to create a smooth paste. Return to pan and stir in wine and tomato paste.

3. Slice bread as thin as possible. Toast one side under the broiler and brush the other with the beef broth. Spread thick with the pâté. Serve at room temperature or place into a 300°F oven for a few minutes to warm.

Note: In Italy, this is called Crostini Di Fegatini, meaning "Little Crusts". They are served on individual plates as an appetizer, garnished with fresh basil leaves.

Mediterranean Linguine with Clams
Linguine alla Vongole
Yield: 2 servings

36 or more Littleneck clams
½ cup Pinot Grigio or
  another dry white wine
2 garlic cloves, minced
2 teaspoons minced fresh
  oregano or 1 teaspoon dried

A sprinkling of red pepper
  flakes or a touch of cayenne
  pepper
½ cup extra virgin Italian
  olive oil
4 tablespoons butter
2 tablespoons rich beef broth

Water
1 tablespoon coarse salt,
  kosher or sea

Flat leaf Italian parsley,
  minced

1. Scrub the clams well under cold, running water. Discard any that are cracked or open that will not close when their shells are tapped.

2. Set them into a large pot with the wine. Cover and bring to a boil. Boil until the shells have opened. Discard any that do not open.
3. Combine the garlic, oregano, pepper flakes, olive oil, butter, and beef broth in a deep skillet. Simmer 15 minutes. Remove the clams from their wine bath and toss with the sauce.
4. Add water and salt to the pot in which the clams cooked. Bring to a boil. Stir in the linguine all at once Cook, stirring often until the pasta is cooked through but still firm. Drain. Do not rinse. Rinsing removes the starch needed to adhere to the sauce. Pour the sauce and clams over and toss.
5. Remove to a serving dish or individual plates.
6. Sprinkle with minced parsley to serve.

Siena's Favorite
Rabbit with Crimini Mushrooms
Coniglio con funghi cremini
Yield: Approximately 4 servings

Cremini mushrooms, named for the Cremini family of Italy, are known as baby bella mushrooms in America. When allowed to fully mature, they become the large mushrooms known as Portobello(a).

1 rabbit, approximately 3 pounds dressed, cut into 10 pieces	2 garlic cloves, minced
	4-5 basil leaves, minced
	1 pound baby bella
Salt and pepper	mushrooms, cleaned, stems
¼ cup Italian olive oil	removed
1 purple onion, chopped fine	1 cup dry white wine
1 tablespoon rosemary, minced	

1 ¼ cups rich chicken broth or 10 ounce can Campbell's® Concentrated Chicken Broth

4 plum tomatoes, seeded and chopped

1. Divide the rabbit into 10 pieces. Sprinkle lightly with salt and pepper.
2. Heat the oil in a deep skillet over medium-high. Sear until the skin turns brown on all sides.
3. Reduce the heat to medium and add the mushrooms. Cook 5 minutes. Toss the rabbit with the onion, rosemary, garlic and basil.
4. Add the wine and broth and bring to a boil. Reduce heat to medium-low and cook, covered, approximately 35-40 minutes or until very tender.
5. Add tomatoes the last 5 minutes.
6. Serve with Tuscan Rice, recipe below

Blackie's Chicken with Tuna
(Pollo di Tonnato)
Yield: 4 servings

This favorite Italian cold dish is the perfect choice for Sunday supper or luncheon. The Italians generally make it with veal (Vitello Tonnato). Chicken breasts are less expensive and just as delicious.

For the Chicken:
4 small chicken breasts, skinned and boned

Salt and pepper

1 onion, sliced thin

2 sage leaves, or 1 teaspoon dried sage

½ cup white wine

½ cup chicken broth

1. Sprinkle the chicken breasts with salt and pepper and set aside. Bring the remaining ingredients to a boil in a deep skillet. Boil, gently, stirring occasionally, 10 minutes. Add the chicken breasts.
2. Reduce heat to low, cover the skillet and cook the breasts approximately 12-15 minutes or until done. Remove the breasts to cool. Strain the broth.
3. Cut the breasts lengthwise to create thin slices. Refrigerate in an airtight container covered with the broth.
   Directly before serving, place the chicken slices on plates or a platter and spread with a thin layer of tonnato.

Tonnato:

6 ounce can of solid white meat Albacore tuna in oil.
Juice from ½ lemon
3 tablespoons bottled capers
3 anchovy fillets
1 teaspoon dill weed
1 tablespoon minced parsley
1 small sweet onion

3 hard-boiled eggs
¼ cup or more mayonnaise to taste
¼ teaspoon salt
¼ teaspoon black pepper
Sliced pimento olives
3 thin sliced hard boiled eggs for the top

1. Drain water from the tuna. Pulverize tuna with lemon juice in a food processor, or chop fine by hand.
2. Combine capers, anchovies, dill, parsley and onion in the processor and pulverize. Mix with the tuna.
3. Pulverize 3 hard-boiled eggs. Mix into the tuna.
4. Stir in mayonnaise. Add salt and pepper to taste. Refrigerate until very cold.
5. Spread a thin layer over chicken breasts. Decorate with olives and sliced eggs.

The Vicar's Custard
Zabaglione
Yield: 4 servings

1 cup fresh chestnuts,
crumbled or mashed
4 jumbo egg yolks
¼ cup Marsala wine
¼ cup granulated sugar

1 cup blueberries,
raspberries, sliced
strawberries, or a
combination
1 ounce dark or semi-sweet
chocolate

For the Chestnuts: Holding a chestnut between your fingers, make a slit across the round side through the skin, being careful not to cut into the flesh of the nut. Cover with water and bring to a boil. Remove from the water and set on a baking sheet. Place into a preheated 350°F oven and roast 35-40 minutes, or until skin has peeled back and chestnut is soft. Remove the skins and crumble the chestnuts.

1. Line 4 dessert bowls or saucer champagne glasses with a layer of the crumbled chestnuts.
2. Separate the eggs, refrigerating the whites for another recipe. (Egg white omelet, meringue cookies, etc.)
3. Set a bowl into a pot half filled with simmering water. Pour in the wine and sugar and beat until just incorporated with a hand electric beater or a wire whisk. Add the egg yolks and vanilla. Continue beating until the mixture becomes very thick.
4. Divide the berries into saucer champagne cups, elegant glasses, or small footed bowls.
5. Spoon the custard over the berries.

6. Shave the chocolate on top and serve immediately.
7. This recipe may be doubled, but it is easier and faster to work it as two recipes. Keep the first covered over warm water until the second is ready to serve.

"For love is as strong as death. Jealousy as cruel as the grave; its flames are flames of fire, A most vehement flame."
— The Holy Bible New King James Version, <u>Song of Solomon</u>, chapter 8.

Susan's Home

Every morning I jump up to Susan's window sill to watch her leave for school. Every afternoon at exactly the same time I return to the sill to wait for her to come home. When her car pulls into the driveway I run to the door. She drops her books and scoops me into her arms to hug me and kiss the top of my head. She never forgets to say how beautiful I am and how much she loves me. These happy times lasted for eight months until she packed up and went off to college. She was my princess and I waited patiently for her return.

Just before Christmas I became aware of an excitement stirring in the house. My love was coming home. *Mom* was in the kitchen making the cheesecake she served to <u>The New York Times</u> Food Editor and cookbook author, Craig Craiborne, when he came to dinner. Susan's favorite breakfasts of oversized Blueberry Muffins and Crêpes filled with cream cheese were prepared in advance to freeze. Chocolate Chip Cookies were packed in a plastic container on the kitchen counter. Cats are not supposed to like sweets but, when the pan of Chocolate Brownies was placed into a 350°F oven, the aroma that filled the entire house and wafted out the door across the front porch into the street had the same effect as catnip. I went to the window in her room looking forward to the joyous moment when I would sleep in that luxuriant hair.

I saw her car as she turned the corner to our street. *Susan is home, Susan is home.* I jumped down from the window sill and ran to greet her at the door. I waited in anticipation for her to hug *mom* and *dad* and then pick me up as she had done every day, but she did not reach down. I moved closer towards her and then stopped dead on my paws when I saw her holding something in her arms. Could it be? I was looking at another white cat, but this time I was not looking into a mirror. It looked like me, but it was smaller and more delicate of bone and its fur was more silken in texture. Remembering my manners, I sat down and raised my paw in a Japanese Bobtail greeting. Susan walked right past me. Neither she nor the cat in her arms looked down. It was as though I didn't exist.

I walked behind them to her room. She set the cat down onto her bed. I jumped up. It made a hissing sound and lashed out with its paw. I didn't back off fast enough and, before I realized what was happening, a sharp pain ran across my cheek. As little droplets of blood appeared, she grabbed the cat and said, "Sakie, leave Hanako alone." She picked me up, dropped me outside her room and closed the door. I walked slowly into the kitchen. *Mom* gathered me into her lap at the breakfast room table. She dabbed at the wound with cool water, and scratched the happy space between my ears until I fell asleep.

Hanako had been given her name by Susan's friend who was majoring in Eastern cultures. It supposedly meant "Flower Child" in Japanese, but this cat was not Japanese. And, she was not of any floral species I wanted in my garden. She did not have to tell me who she was. I recognized her immediately. Although she was not as old a spirit as I, her blood line was at one time impeccable. There was no denying her country of origin. She had been a Turkish Angora, brought to Europe from Ankara in the 1600's during the Holy Wars. Her name, Angora, actually was another spelling of the city of Ankara.

The Angora is known to be a sweet cat that adores its owner and shows its affection. It is also more stubborn than any cat I have known. Once it makes up its mind, that's that. Hanako made up her mind she was going to disgrace me so she would be the only cat acceptable to the family.

She put her scheme into motion the first day *mom* and *dad* left the house. Susan was washing her hair and couldn't hear what was about to unfold in the living room.

Bet you can't catch me, she purred.

She ran around me in a circle before jumping from chair to chair, onto the tables and finally to the Steinway baby grand piano where she ran up and down the keys creating tinkling sounds that resounded through the room. I immediately gave chase. I bounded down the piano keys in close pursuit racing close enough to be whipped by her tail. Suddenly she sprang from the keys upward to the sounding board, her narrow body barely clearing the space between the French Baccarat crystal girandole and the music desk. I leaped after her, vaguely aware of sheet music flying and the sound of crashing glass as the girandole fell into a million pieces below. She scooted into Susan's room and wedged her way through the narrow crack of the door into the bathroom.

Susan found me sitting on top of the piano looking bewildered at the pile of glass on the floor. The mate to the broken museum piece remained regal of posture on the other platform of the piano desk, thereby drawing further attention to the empty space. She swept up the glass, keeping the large piece that had been the base in hopes mom could do something with it. She didn't accuse me. She knew instinctively what had happened. The disheveled condition of the living room gave enough evidence of our charade.

When *mom* saw what had happened, she didn't want Susan to think it was her fault. She picked up the remaining girandole and placed it on a small table on the opposite side of the room. Standing back, she admired it carefully and said,

"It looks quite lovely here."

Cheesecake for Craig and Susan
Yield: 9-10 X 4 inch spring-form pan

32 ounces (4- 8 ounce packages) cream cheese, softened to room temperature
5 jumbo egg yolks, room temperature
1 ¼ cup granulated sugar
2 teaspoons vanilla extract
2 tablespoons orange juice

2 tablespoons lime juice
7 tablespoons sour cream
¼ cup all-purpose flour
5 jumbo egg whites, room temperature or warmer
¼ teaspoon cream of tartar
1 tablespoon granulated sugar
9-inch spring form pan

1. Preheat the oven to 450°F.
2. Beat the cream cheese on high speed of an electric mixer for 10 seconds. Add the sugar and continue to beat until fluffy. Turn off mixer and scrape the sides and bottom of the bowl. Lower the speed to medium and add the egg yolks, one at a time, turning the mixer off after the second yolk has been added to scrape the sides and bottom.
3. Add vanilla and fruit juices on low speed. Add the s our cream. Add the flour. Scrape the sides and bottom and turn the mixer on high speed for 3-4 seconds.
4. Beat the egg whites in a separate bowl on high speed until foamy. Add cream of tartar and beat until thick. Add sugar and continue beating until smooth.
5. Fold beaten whites into the cream cheese mixture and pour into the springform pan. Set the rack one-third from the bottom of the oven and bake the cake for 6 minutes, or until the top begins to turn color. Reduce heat immediately to

250°F and continue baking another 40 minutes. Turn off the oven and open the door to cool.

6. Refrigerate overnight, or freeze, tightly covered. Top with fresh fruit glazed with strawberry or apple jelly, or a chocolate frosting.

Amaretto Cheesecake: Exchange the vanilla for 2 teaspoons almond extract or Amaretto liqueur.

Old Fashioned Blueberry Muffins
Yield: 12 normal size 2" round or 6 huge muffins 4" round

2 cups all-purpose flour	1 cup granulated sugar
2 teaspoons baking powder	2 jumbo eggs
½ teaspoon cinnamon	2 teaspoons vanilla extract
½ teaspoon salt	½ cup fat-free half and half
¼ pound butter, softened	2 cups fresh blueberries

1. Preheat oven to 350°F.
2. Sift together the flour, baking powder, cinnamon and salt.
3. Cream the butter and sugar in a bowl, beating at least 5 minutes, scraping the sides several times.
4. Add the eggs, one at a time, beating after each addition, scraping the sides several times.
5. Add the vanilla.
6. Add ½ the flour, beating on low speed to incorporate.
7. Add ½ the half and half, beating on low speed to incorporate.
8. Add remaining flour and half and half. Scrape the sides between each addition.
9. Fold in the blueberries
10. Spray the muffin cups with vegetable oil or insert paper holders.

11. Fill the muffin cups all the way to the top.
12. Bake ⅓ from the bottom of the oven 25-30 minutes for normal size and 40-45 minutes for 3" round. Check by inserting a toothpick.
Note: Exchange or add raspberries, peaches, strawberries, or any other fresh fruit of choice, except melon.

Sweet Crêpes
For breakfast or dessert crêpes or roll-ups
Yield: Approximately 18-20

4 jumbo eggs	1½ cups cold milk
1 full teaspoon granulated sugar	¾ cup cold water
	4 tablespoons melted butter
¼ teaspoon salt	6-inch shallow non-stick
1 full teaspoon vanilla	crêpe pan or round skillet
2 ½ cups all-purpose flour, sifted	

1. Beat eggs with a wire whisk or hand-held beater, stirring clockwise and counter-clockwise to smooth the batter evenly.
2. Add sugar, salt and vanilla.
3. Stir in half the flour. Stir in all the milk. Stir in remaining flour. Stir in the water.
4. Cover and allow mixture to sit 30 minutes.
5. Strain into another bowl.
6. Stir in the melted butter. Allow mixture to stand at room temperature 15 minutes.
7. Stir and pour into a cup with a spout.

8. Heat a non-stick frying pan or crêpe pan (8 inches inside dimension) over medium heat. Pour in enough batter to cover the bottom and, as it sticks, immediately pour the extra batter back into the cup, leaving a thin layer in the pan. When the batter has partially set, run a butter knife around the side where the batter has been poured to remove excess batter that has adhered to the side of the pan.

9. If the crêpe is too thick (pancake), stir another ¼ cup water into the batter.

10. Cook on one side until slightly browned but not hard. This should take approximately 30 seconds. You will see small bubbles at the edges. Flip the crêpe upside down onto wax paper. As crêpes cool, stack them on a large piece of wax paper.

11. When finished, fold the paper over to cover until ready to fill.

Note: Do not forget to strain the batter. This is very important.

If the crêpes are not going to be filled until the following day, set them into a tightly closed container in the refrigerator. These freeze beautifully for several months in an airtight container

Cheese Filling for Sweet Breakfast Crêpes
This recipe will fill 18-eight inch crêpes

15 ounces Farmer's cheese or small curd cottage cheese

16 ounces cream cheese (2-8 ounce packages)

3 jumbo or 4 extra large egg yolks

½ teaspoon cinnamon (or more to taste)

Optional: Pinch of nutmeg

1 tablespoon granulated sugar (less or more to taste)

Pinch of salt

2 teaspoons vanilla extract

Optional: 2 tablespoons freshly squeezed orange juice

Sour cream, fresh berries and jam at the table

1. Combine the Farmer's cheese with the cream cheese and beat until smooth with a hand electric beater. Add remaining ingredients and beat well.
2. Spoon 2 tablespoons of the cheese mixture in the center of the un-cooked side of each crêpe. Fold one flap over the filling. Working around in a circle, fold the one next to it over it and then the 3rd and 4th to create a square.
3. Set the blintzes flap-side down in a small amount of clarified butter in a non-stick skillet. Turn when brown and cook the other side. Remove to paper toweling to remove any grease.
4. Serve with sour cream or crème fraîche and a side dish of fresh strawberries or blueberries or strawberry jam, blueberry jam, or yogurt with fruit.

Note: To Freeze: Set the cheese filled crêpes on a baking sheet covered with parchment or wax paper. Freeze 2 hours. Cover tightly or slip into a plastic container. Don't forget to label with the date. Directly before serving, remove the crêpes from the freezer, set them on individual plates covered with plastic wrap, and microwave one minute.

Crème Fraîche
Yield: 3 cups

This succulent invention of the French has a flavor all its own, and can be used instead of sour cream as a garnish. It is particularly marvelous over breakfast cheese crêpes and roll-ups. Try a dollop on top of tomato based soups.

2 cups heavy whipping cream   ⅓ cup sour cream
⅔ cup whole buttermilk

1. Combine the cream and buttermilk in a large glass container. Place into the microwave on high for 30 seconds. Stir. Test by dropping a small amount on the inside of your wrist. When the temperature is lukewarm (90-100°F), it is ready. If too cool, microwave again another 10 seconds. Stir again and test.
2. Cover and set in a warm place for 8 hours, or until it begins to thicken. Stir in sour cream. Refrigerate until very cold.
   Note: This will remain until the expiration date of the milk and cream.
   Remove from the refrigerator directly before serving. Room temperature will cause it to lose thickness.
   The recipe for Gr. Marnier Dessert Crêpes is the same as Sweet Crêpes, with the addition of orange juice and Gr. Marnier liqueur. It is best to make these in a 6-inch pan, if available. The smaller pan will yield approximately 24 crêpes.

Gr. Marnier Dessert Crêpes

Fill with raspberry, strawberry, or blueberry jam or fresh fruit
Serve with whipped cream or vanilla ice cream

1. Beat eggs with a wire whisk or hand-held beater. Add sugar, salt, vanilla, plus 1 tablespoon fresh orange juice, and 2 tablespoons Gr. Marnier liqueur.
2. Stir in half the flour. Stir in all the milk. Stir in remaining flour. Stir in the water.
3. Cover and allow mixture to sit 30 minutes.
4. Strain into another bowl.
5. Stir in the melted butter. Allow mixture to stand at room temperature 15 minutes.
6. Stir and pour into a cup with a spout.
7. Heat a non-stick frying pan or crêpe pan (6 inches inside dimension) over medium heat. Pour in enough batter to cover the bottom and, as it sticks, immediately pour the extra batter back into the cup, leaving a thin layer in the pan. When the batter has partially set, run a butter knife around the side where the batter has been poured to remove excess batter that has adhered to the side of the pan.
8. Cook on one side until slightly browned but not hard. This should take approximately 30 seconds. You will see small bubbles at the edges. Flip the crêpe upside down onto wax paper. As crêpes cool, stack them on a large piece of wax paper.
9. When finished, fold the paper over to cover the crêpes.
10. Toss thinly sliced fresh peaches, strawberries, raspberries, or blueberries with cinnamon-sugar (1 part cinnamon to 7 parts granulated sugar). Spoon along the center of the crêpe

and cover with one side. Then cover with the other to create an oblong. Cover until ready to serve.

11. Marinate more fruit in a little cinnamon-sugar, tossing with Gr. Marnier or liqueur of choice.

Note: These may be set on a serving plate, covered with plastic wrap and microwaved for 30 seconds to serve.

ROLL-UPS can be made for breakfast or dessert: Toss thinly sliced fresh peaches, strawberries, raspberries, or blueberries with cinnamon-sugar. Spoon across the center of the crêpe and fold one side over. Roll or fold the other to create an oblong. Cover until ready to serve.

Apple Filling for Roll-Ups
Yield: 8 or more crêpes

Most recipes call for Rome or Granny Smith apples. Fiji and Ambrosia are naturally sweeter and require less sugar.

6 large Fiji or Ambrosia
  apples
½ cup unsalted butter
⅓ cup granulated sugar
1 teaspoon cinnamon
½ cup thinly slivered almonds
  or chopped pecans

Sifted powdered sugar to
  sprinkle
Optional ½ cup amaretto
  (almond), frangelico
  (hazelnut) or apple liqueur.

1. Peel and cut the apples into small squares or thin slices.
2. Sauté in the butter over very low heat, stirring often, until soft.
3. Combine the sugar and cinnamon and sprinkle over the apples, stirring until mixed.

4. Spoon the mixture along the center of each crêpe. Cover the apples with one side of the crêpe and roll to create a log.
5. Sprinkle with almonds or pecans.
6. Divide on plates and sprinkle with powdered sugar.
   Note: The crêpes can be filled several hours in advance, covered, and microwaved 40 seconds before adding the nuts and sugar to serve hot. For a dinner dessert, heat the liqueur to the boiling point. Ignite. Set crêpes into the pan and spoon the liqueur over to serve.

Susan's Home
Chocolate Chip Cookies
Yield: Approximately 36 cookies

2 ¼ cups sifted all-purpose flour
1 scant teaspoon baking soda
¼ teaspoon salt
¾ cup granulated sugar
¾ cup packed light brown sugar
1 cup ½ pound) butter, softened

2 jumbo eggs
1 full tablespoon plus 1 teaspoon vanilla extract
18 ounces semi-sweet chocolate chips
Optional: 1 cup chopped walnuts or pecans

1. Preheat oven to 350°F.
2. Sift the flour with the soda and salt. Set aside.
3. Combine white and brown sugars with the butter and beat on highest speed of an electric mixer until white and creamy. Scrape bowl several times during the mixing.
4. Beat in eggs, one at a time. Scrape sides.
5. Add vanilla.- Add flour mixture until blended. Scrape sides.

6. Stir in chocolate chips and nuts, if desired.
7. Cover a baking sheet with parchment paper. With a tablespoon, drop cookie batter one-inch apart. Flatten each cookie slightly with the back of the spoon.
8. Bake 15-18 minutes for large cookies, 12-14 minutes for smaller ones, depending upon your choice of soft or crisp cookies.

Better than Catnip Brownies
Yield: 8 or 9 inch square pan

2 tablespoons unsweetened cocoa
1 ¼ cups all-purpose flour, sifted
½ teaspoon salt
6 ounces semi-sweet chocolate
¼ cup water
1 tablespoon vanilla extract
1 cup butter (½ pound), softened

6 ounces cream cheese, softened
1½ cups granulated sugar
2 tablespoons mayonnaise
3 jumbo graded eggs (or 4 extra-large)
Optional: Mini chocolate chips for the top
8 or 9 inch square baking pan (You can use disposable)

1. Preheat oven to 350°F.
2. Sift the cocoa, flour and salt together and set aside.
3. Melt the chocolate with the water in a small pot over lowest heat. Stir and add the vanilla.
4. Beat the butter, cream cheese and sugar on high speed of an electric mixer until white and fluffy. Scrape the sides of the bowl with a spatula. Add the mayonnaise on medium speed.

5. Beat in the eggs, one at a time on medium speed, scraping the bowl each time. Add the melted chocolate mixture.
6. Beat in the flour mixture all at once on low speed.
7. Spoon the batter into the pan. Bake 30 minutes, and test for doneness with a wood skewer. The batter should be slightly wet. If still liquid, cook another 5 minutes to check again. Do not over-bake. These are best when very moist.
8. Remove from the oven and immediately cover the top with mini chocolate chips.

   Note: The size and material of the baking pan makes a difference in the cooking time. Also, if you bake in disposable aluminum pans, the cooking time decreases.

"A cat may look at a king"
— English Proverb

Le Chat de Madame Royale

THE NEXT DAY WHILE I was sleeping in the rays of sun that streamed through the kitchen window, Hanako approached me.

Come to Susan's room. I want to tell you about myself.

She jumped on the bed and curled into a comfortable position. I followed, more from curiosity than interest.

O.K. but make it short. You've brought enough trouble into my life already.

I have come from a renowned French bloodline. I am descended from the cat presented to the powerful Cardinal Richelieu in 1630. I also was the white cat sitting at the feet of Louis XIV in the portrait painted during his reign of 1643-1715.

I looked at her out of one eye, letting her know she was disturbing my nap. And then she said something that truly interested me.

I was born again in 1788 to the Court of Marie Antoinette and Louis XVI and survived the French

Revolution with their eldest daughter, Madame Royale.

This made me take notice. I picked up my head. Being a history buff, I asked if she would relate her life with Marie Antoinette so I would know what had happened during that ill-fated time.

King Louis XIV, known as the Grand Monarch or Sun King, reigned over France fifty-four years. He, like other noble families of his time, was infatuated with the Turkish Angora cat, that he called an 'ethereal breed'. We were even allowed to roam about the tables during court gatherings.

She saw that I was about to tell her I was an Angora cat, and raised her paw. As she carefully studied me, I sat with my head up. The tips of my beautiful pink ears formed perfect points, and my front legs stood in a straight line from my body to the floor. I swished my long bushy tail and turned my elegant Egyptian head to show my profile.

You're pretty, but your fur is too woolly and your ears are too small and your snout does not come to a point the way it should. No, Sakie. You are a typical example of what happened to my breed when it was mixed with other longhairs in France, England and America. People today call any long-haired, white cat Angora, but the only pure Angora is the Turkish that traces its ancestry all the way back to Ankara (Angora), Turkey, where it was domesticated by the Chinese and bred with long-haired cats from Asia.

The Turkish people believed that these long-haired white cats with blue eyes or 'odd-eyes' (one blue eye and one eye of another color) brought good fortune to the owner. In the late 1600's, a man named Nicolas Claude Fabri de Pereisc brought my ancestors to France where he bred them for the aristocracy, who considered them objects of good fortune and a sign of luxury. You are the offspring of crossbreeding with Persian and Afghan cats.

The little snob was making me angry but I decided to listen to her anyway.

I was only four weeks old when they brought me to Louis XIV but my silky coat was shining and my body was long with fine bone structure with the promise of firm muscle. My huge ears set into my tiny head were already pointed and tufted, resting close together in an erect stance. What endeared him to me, however, were my eyes that were large and perfectly almond shaped, slanting slightly upward. And, whereas my breed had many eye colors ranging from copper, golden, and green-golden to odd-eyed, the most precious color was blue. My eyes were the color of the very sky itself. He became so attached to me that he had me join the family portrait to play at the feet of his great-grandchild, the future Louis XV. Louis XV became king when he was only five years old after his father died from gangrene of the leg in 1715. Louis XV had several Turkish Angoras during his lifetime, but his favorite was my beautiful granddaughter that he named 'Brilliant'.

Le Chat de Madame Royale

I was born again in 1788 to please the children of his great-grandson, Louis XVI and the self-indulgent Marie Antoinette.

I was becoming terribly confused.

Who are all these Louis people? Why didn't they have their own names? I only count three kings. You have four kings named Louis and the fifth the Louis XVI about whom you want to tell your story.

That's because so many people died from smallpox and measles in those days. Even royal families lost most of their children because they had no medicines to cure them. Did you know that Louis XIV could eat four plates of soup, a whole pheasant, a partridge, a huge salad, mutton smothered with gravy, two slices of ham, and a whole plate of pastry at just one meal? And, he ate with his fingers rather than with forks that had been invented a hundred years before in Italy. He also forbade his family or courtiers to use the fork. He was called the Sun King, but during the great famine of 1705-1708 when the people were dying of starvation, he became the most hated king France had known. When he died they performed an autopsy and found that his stomach was two times normal size with an enormous tapeworm living inside.

A sound like 'yuk' emerged from my throat before I could silence it. She raised her paw to show me her scissor sharp claws and hissed

If you will stop interrupting me, I will go on. Until Louis XV reached maturity, the French were ruled by the Duke of Orléans as Regent. When Louis took over he was at first called Louis the Well-Beloved. But then he began to lose wars and have huge fights with his Court and Parliament, and he created religious conflict. They said it was he who was the cause of the Revolution rather than his inept son, Louis XVI.

The tragic figure in this story was beautiful Marie Antoinette. I was truly the only one that pitied the young Queen who had been named Antonia by her loving mother, the Empress Maria Theresa of Austria. Her childhood was so very happy. When she was thirteen, the exuberant cameo-skinned, fair-haired Archduchess played childish games in the palace with the young musical prodigy, Mozart. Then, in 1770, immediately following her fourteenth birthday and announcement of her womanhood, she was shipped off to France to marry the fat, awkward, impotent fifteen year-old grandson heir to the throne of Louis XV. The doomed pair suddenly became King and Queen four years later when Louis XV died from smallpox. When Louis XVI was told he was the King of France, the wail of the teenagers echoed off the palace walls for all to hear: "Protect us Lord, for we are too young to reign." *Without a clue as to what was expected of them, they entertained themselves with lavish balls and indulged themselves with material possessions. It seems as though the young king had*

*an operation to enable his manhood to come forth
and their first child, Marie Therese Charlotte, called
Madame Royale, was born in 1778. The second
child, a weakly son, Louis Joseph known as M. Le
Dauphin, was born in 1781, but died in 1789.
Another daughter, Princess Sophia, born in 1786,
died before her first birthday. The Prince Royal,
Louis XVII was born in 1785.*

Fearfully, I interrupted again.

*Hanako, I said, this history lesson is very interesting,
but could you get on with it? It's almost time for me
to go to the kitchen to see what mom's brewing for
supper.*

*Keep quiet and listen to me! You cross-breeds are all
the same. You have no patience. I will now begin
my story.*

*I was brought to the Palace of Versailles for inspection
in 1788 when I was six weeks old. I was the most
beautiful of the entire litter of pure pedigree Turkish
Angoras. Madame Royale had just celebrated her
tenth birthday. She was lovely to behold, with a
charming smile and the elegant composure of a true
princess. The Prince Royal was only three. Marie
Antoinette carried me to the portrait of King Louis
XIV to show the children they had been given a
cat exactly like the one in the painting. They all
marveled at my appearance.*

"She is perfect", exclaimed the thirty-two year-old queen.

The children were then prescribed explicit instructions on caring for a royal cat. As they listened, I tried to focus on my surroundings. The long corridor was completely covered with mirrors that duplicated everything so many times I could not tell how many people were there. I squinted at the lights that bounced off the mirrors from dozens of dazzling crystal chandeliers. My eyes tried to focus on the hundreds of Sèvres porcelain vases lined up in front of the mirrors, but they were a blur of gold and blue and green and red. I had indeed found a magnificent home.

During the next year the children combed my long, shining hair four times each day. They dressed me in remnants of extra silk from their best clothing sewn by the royal seamstress for their appearances at court. They made up stories with me as the heroine. Sometimes I was a princess kidnapped by peasants who demanded ransom from the royal guards who wanted the beautiful princess saved. At other times I was myself, Le Chat Royal, who somehow got out of the palace and couldn't find her way back. They would hide me in the pantry and then pretend to look for me. When they found me, they always feigned great surprise and joy as they held hands and danced in a circle around me. They were good children, naïve and spoiled like their parents, but genuinely loving and kind. Although I always showed affection to the Dauphin Royal Prince and the Queen and King, my gentle disposition then, as it is now, was to bond with only one person. Madame Royale and I became inseparable. I loved her as much as any cat could love a human person. She, like Susan in this life, doted on me as though I were her child.

As a privileged feline I joined the royal family at their table. Tender veal medallions sautéed with vegetables and tomatoes called "chasseur", and roasted duckling from Nantes accompanied by crêpes filled with fresh asparagus covered with hollandaise sauce were portioned on small Sevres and Limoges porcelain plates and set on the floor next to Madame Royale's chair. They even shared marvelous custard they called Crème Brûlée after removing the crusty sugar topping because they knew cats didn't like sugar. But the "pièce de résistance" was a dessert they called "profiteroles". They were fashioned from dough called pate à choux that was baked into delicate puffs and filled with a pastry cream called "crème patisserie". They were served very cold covered in warm rich chocolate sauce.

Little did we know that my favorite appetizer of the succulent combination of a paste made from finely chopped liver with cognac they called pâté was to be Queen Marie's last meal before she was taken from the Tower to have her head cut off by the guillotine.

I did not want to interrupt but could not help myself.

But, why, I asked, *what had they done wrong?*

She continued as though I had not spoken.

You see, Sakie, the problem was that the privileged few of France seemed unaware that the people they passed in the streets every day went to bed every night with their stomachs hurting from hunger or that they lived in darkness after the sun set when we had enough candles to light every house in Paris. When Queen Marie and Louis spent their summers in Versailles, the people gathered outside the windows of their summer home at Le Petit Trianon Palace to watch the Royal family and their court feast on rich soup made from fresh shellfish brought in from Marseilles followed by the white meat of chicken cooked in creamy wine sauce and tiny pancakes called crêpes filled with fresh strawberries while they subsisted on gruel and discarded stale bread. When the King and Queen were told of the misery of their subjects, they felt no social conscience or empathy because they did not understand.

For a moment she stopped talking. Then, a low growl came from her throat and her green eyes slanted into tiny slits as she recounted the horror that followed.

Summer Soup at Versailles
Yield: 4-6 servings

True Bouillabaisse should be created from the fish that swim off the Marseilles coast of France. The recipe below incorporates fish from American waters.
Purchase fresh fish from a fish market that will fillet them while you wait.

Shellfish:

18 mussels – To clean: Place into a pan. Cover with cold water. Sprinkle 1 teaspoon dry mustard over. Scrub under cold water. Discard any that are open and do not close when tapped. Place washed mussels in a pan with:
1 thinly sliced onion, 1 thinly sliced celery rib, 1 bay leaf, and 1 cup dry white wine. Add ½ cup water, ¼ teaspoon white pepper, and 1 teaspoon sea salt. Cover the pan. Bring to a boil. Shake until mussels open. Remove the mussels. Discard the top shell from each mussel. Cover the mussels and set aside. Strain the broth.
6 cold water lobster tails, 4-5 ounces each: cut into the back shell and remove the vein. Cut into halves cross-wise. Combine 4 tablespoons butter with 2 tablespoons vegetable oil in a heavy pan over medium heat. Add the lobster tails. Cover the pan and cook 3 minutes. Add ¼ cup brandy or cognac. Bring to a boil and cook, spooning the sauce over, until the shells turn bright red. Remove the tails. Combine the broth with that from the mussels.

SAUCE:

4 tablespoons butter

2 cloves garlic, minced

4 beefsteak tomatoes, skinned, seeded and cut into small cubes

1 tablespoon tomato paste

Strained broth from the mussels and lobster

Salt and a touch of white pepper to taste

FISH:

4 fillets of sole or flounder, rolled and tied

4 fillets of bass, rolled and tied

1 medium-size red snapper, skinned, boned, and cut into 4 fillets

½ pound medium size raw shrimp (30-40 per pound), shelled and deveined

1 pound sea scallops

1. Combine the sauce ingredients in a deep skillet. Bring to a boil, stirring. Add the fish. Reduce heat to medium-low. Cook, spooning sauce over the fish until the fish turn white and are done.
2. Reduce heat to simmer. Stir in the shrimp and scallops and reserved mussels and lobster and cover to cook no longer than 5 minutes. Remove the skillet from the heat and leave covered until ready to serve when it can be reheated over a low fire.

Serve in large soup plates or pasta dishes over fried croutons.

Fried Croutons

Slice a loaf of French bread into thick slices (1-inch). Sprinkle with powdered or pulverized saffron on one side. Heat vegetable oil only to cover the bottom of a non- stick skillet. Set the slices saffron side down and brown. Sprinkle the top with saffron and turn to brown. Set in the bottom of the soup plate and ladle the soup over.

The French Hunter's Choice Veau Chausseur
Yield: 4 servings

Any sauce with the addition of tomatoes or tomato paste is called "hunter" in French and Italian recipes. Chasseur is the French word for hunter. In Italian, it is cacciatore.

2 pounds veal tenderloin
Flour to coat
1 tablespoon unsalted butter
  mixed with 2 tablespoons
  extra virgin olive oil
2 tablespoons unsalted butter
1 large clove garlic, minced
1 large shallot, finely diced
½ cup finely diced carrots

½ pound thinly sliced baby
  bella mushrooms
1 tablespoon flour
½ cup dry white wine
1 ¼ cups beef broth
2 tablespoons tomato paste
Salt and pepper
Minced large leaf parsley

1. Slice the tenderloin into 4 medallions approximately ¼ inch thick and cut each into cubes of equal proportion to yield 4 servings.
2. Sauté garlic, shallot, carrots and mushrooms in the butter in a saucepan over low heat until soft. (Carrots will still be firm)

3. Add flour. Stir in wine and broth and cook over medium heat until thickened. Stir in tomato paste over very low heat.
4. Sprinkle veal pieces with salt and pepper. Coat the veal with the flour, shaking off excess.
5. Combine the butter and oil in a shallow sauté pan. When the mixture begins to bubble, set the veal cubes in and cook quickly over medium-high heat until brown on both sides. Do not overcook.
6. Remove to a serving platter or individual plates and spoon sauce over. Sprinkle minced parsley on top to serve immediately.

Note: The sauce may be made in advance.

Louis' Creamed Chicken
Yield: 6 servings

For The Chicken:

2-3 chicken breasts, rib bones attached for a strong broth
Salt, black pepper
2 cups water
½ cup dry white wine
1 small onion, sliced
1 rib celery, sliced
⅛ teaspoon nutmeg
Roasting pan

1. Preheat oven to 350°F.
2. Sprinkle chicken breasts with salt and pepper.
3. Combine remaining ingredients in a roasting pan. Cook the chicken breasts, covered, approximately 35 minutes, or until tender. Cool in the broth 30 minutes.
4. Remove breasts. Strain broth. It should yield approximately 2 cups.

For The Sauce:

2 tablespoons butter
½ pound white mushrooms,
  sliced
2 tablespoons butter
3 tablespoons all-purpose
  flour
Broth from the chicken

2 tablespoons sweet cream
  sherry
⅓ cup half and half (half
  milk-half cream)
¼ cup heavy cream
10 ounce package frozen
  green peas, thawed
Medium-size pot

1. Sauté the mushrooms in 2 tablespoons butter over medium heat until they are done to your liking. Sprinkle lightly with salt and pepper. Transfer to a bowl.
2. Melt 2 tablespoons butter in the pan from the mushrooms. Stir in the flour.
3. Slowly add the broth over medium heat, stirring until smooth and thickened. Stir in the wine. Stir in the half and half. Return the mushrooms to the pan. Stir in the heavy cream. Stir in the peas. Remove from the heat.
4. Remove the bones from the chicken breasts and slice the meat or cut into cubes.
5. Stir into the sauce.
6. Serve over toast points or in puff pastry shells.

Duckling from Nantes
Yield: 4 servings

For The Sauce:

½ cup red currant jelly
½ cup dry white wine
2 ounces Crème de Cassis
   liqueur

½ cup chicken broth
2 tablespoons Arrowroot
   dissolved in ¼ cup cool water
½ pint blackberries

1. Combine the jelly, wine, liqueur, and broth in a saucepan and heat to the boiling point. Reduce heat to low. Stir in the arrowroot mixture, cooking over low heat until thickened. Stir in the blackberries and remove from the heat.

For The Duck:

4 boneless duck breasts, ¾
   pound each, skin on
Salt, pepper
2 tablespoons clarified
   unsalted butter

1 pint blackberries
2 tablespoons Crème de
   Cassis liqueur

1. Preheat oven to 350ºF.
2. Score the skin in several places. Do not cut into the meat.
3. Sprinkle the breasts lightly with salt and pepper on both sides.
4. Bring the butter to the bubbly point in a skillet and set them skin side down.
5. Cook over medium heat approximately 10 minutes, pouring off any fat as it is released. When the skin is brown and crisp, turn the breasts over. Cover the skillet and cook one minute only, just to seal in the juices.

6. Remove to a shallow baking pan, skin side up, and cook in the oven 5 minutes only. Remove from the oven to rest another 5 minutes.
7. Toss blackberries in Crème de Cassis and arrange around the outside of plates. Pour sauce over the breasts and serve over baked or boiled sweet potatoes, mashed with butter and salt.

Asparagus Crêpes with Hollandaise Sauce
Yield: 4 servings

16-20 asparagus, depending on thickness
Salt

2 tablespoons melted clarified butter

1. Clarify the butter and set aside in a warm place.
2. Put the heads of the asparagus spears together so they will be the same length when served, cut off the bottoms at the point where the color changes to green. Discard bottoms.
3. Pour 1 inch water into a deep skillet, just to cover asparagus spears. Bring to a hard boil. Cover. Boil 1 minute only for thin asparagus, 2 minutes only for medium, 3 minutes only for thick stalks. Remove from the heat immediately. Pour off water. Cover with ice cubes. Remove ice after 5 minutes. Sprinkle asparagus with salt. Brush with clarified butter.
4. Set 4-5 asparagus on the center of each crêpe. Fold one side over. Fold the other side over to create an oblong pocket for the asparagus. Remove to a covered microwavable platter.
5. Make Hollandaise Sauce and keep warm.
6. Microwave asparagus crêpes 20 seconds only.
7. Spoon Hollandaise sauce over to serve.

Clarified Butter

Unsalted butter is best for clarified butter. You lose approximately one-third of the volume when you separate the milk solids, so gauge amounts before clarifying. Below are three methods.

STOVETOP METHOD

Melt butter in a small saucepan. Bring just to the bubbly point, but do not boil. Remove from the stove and skim off the top foam. Allow to stand until lukewarm, and, either strain through cheesecloth or a fine sieve. Or pour off as much yellow liquid as possible, leaving the white milk solids at the bottom. You can also refrigerate the clarified butter as is and remove the yellow top when solidified, warming it before use.

OVEN METHOD

Put the butter into a small dish and melt at 325°F until it begins to bubble. Remove from the oven to cool and follow the directions for the Stove Top Method.

MICROWAVE METHOD

This is easiest of all. Put the butter into a glass cup. Lightly cover and microwave on high for 30 seconds. Pour off the yellow clarified butter and discard the milk solids.

Hollandaise Sauce
Yield: 1 full cup
Recipe can be doubled

5 jumbo egg yolks
½ teaspoon salt
⅛ teaspoon white pepper
½ pound clarified butter
  (½ pound + 5 tablespoons

unsalted butter). Directions
above
2 tablespoons strained lemon
juice

1. Combine yolks, salt and white pepper in the top of a double boiler or in a bowl over simmering but not boiling water.
2. Whisk until very foamy.
3. Add the butter, 1 tablespoon at a time, whisking until mixture thickens. Do not allow the water under the sauce to boil at any time or sauce will curdle.
4. Remove from the heat. Whisk in the lemon juice. Taste for seasonings. Add a pinch of cayenne, if you like.
5. Remove from the heat. Keep the sauce covered over the water until ready to serve. Do not reheat.

Crêpes for Asparagus
Yield: 15-18 pancakes
These freeze beautifully, tightly covered

4 jumbo eggs
1 jumbo egg yolk
¼ teaspoon salt
1½ cups cold milk
½ cup cold water

2 ½ cups all-purpose flour,
  sifted
4 tablespoons melted butter
6-inch shallow non-stick
  crêpe pan or round or
  square shallow skillet

1. Beat eggs with salt with a wire whisk or hand-held beater.
2. Stir in half the flour. Stir in all the milk. Stir in remaining flour. Stir in the water.
3. Cover and allow mixture to sit 30 minutes.
4. Strain into another bowl.
5. Stir in the melted butter. Allow mixture to stand at room temperature 15 minutes.
6. Stir and pour into a cup with a spout.
7. Heat a non-stick frying pan or crêpe pan (6 inches inside dimension) over medium heat. Pour in enough batter to cover the bottom and, as it sticks, immediately pour the extra batter back into the cup, leaving a thin layer in the pan. When the batter has partially set, run a butter knife around the side where the batter has been poured to remove excess batter that has adhered to the side of the pan.
8. Cook on one side until slightly browned but not hard. This should take approximately 30 seconds. You will see small bubbles at the edges. Flip the crêpe upside down onto wax paper. As crêpes cool, stack them on a large piece of wax paper.
9. When finished, fold the paper over to cover the crêpes.

Crème Brûlée
Yield: 4 servings

1 pint heavy cream
6 jumbo egg yolks
½ cup granulated sugar
2 teaspoons vanilla
4 crème brûlée dishes
(shallow round porcelain

baking dishes) or 1 quart
shallow baking dish
½ cup packed light brown
sugar
¼ cup granulated sugar

1. Preheat oven to 350°F.
2. Heat the cream almost to the boiling point. Do not allow it to boil. Remove from the stove.
3. Beat the egg yolks and sugar until blended with a wire whisk. Pour the hot cream over them a little at a time, beating in well.
4. Add the vanilla.
5. Place the individual dishes on a baking sheet with sides. Pour water into the baking sheet to reach ¼ up their sides so the custard will not burn on the bottom.
6. Pour the custard through a strainer into the dishes.
7. Bake 35-40 minutes until firm when a knife inserted comes out clean. Do not overbake.
8. Refrigerate until very cold.

For the Sugar Topping: After baking the custards, turn off the oven. Combine the brown and granulated sugars and spread on a baking sheet lined with parchment paper. Set it into the oven for 1 hour to dry out the sugars.

To Serve: Sprinkle the sugar over the cold custards. Brown the sugar with a kitchen blow torch or set directly under the broiler to brown. The sugar will harden. Serve immediately.

Profiteroles

Cream Puffs (Pâte à Choux)
Food processor method
Yield: Approximately 24 small or 12 large puffs

¼ pound unsalted butter
¼ teaspoon salt
¼ teaspoon granulated sugar
1 scant cup water
½ teaspoon vanilla

1 level cup all-purpose flour
3 extra-large or jumbo eggs
Baking sheet
Parchment paper

1. Preheat oven to 350°F.
2. Melt the butter in a small pot. Add the salt and sugar. Add the water and vanilla and bring to a complete boil, stirring, until mixture begins to foam.

   Remove the pot from the stove. Add the flour immediately, all at once, stirring hard in circular motion with a wooden spoon. Use the spoon to form the mixture into a large ball, bringing all the particles from the sides of the pot into it. It will resemble mashed potatoes. Set aside covered with wax paper to cool.

   Place the ball into the food processor with the steel blade and turn on-off for just a second. Add the 3 eggs all at once. Turn the machine on and count to 10. Turn off. Turn on again and count to 20. When it is quite firm, it is ready. If the batter is still watery, turn the machine on again for 10 seconds.
3. Cover the baking sheet with parchment paper. Drop the batter by either teaspoon or tablespoon, depending upon the size desired.

4. Bake 20-30 minutes, or until puffed and medium brown. Watch carefully. If you remove them from the oven too soon, they will collapse. If you cook them too long, they will be hard.
5. Remove them from the oven and, as soon as they are cool enough to manage, split them horizontally with a small serrated knife.
6. Fill with whipped cream or Crème Patisserie and cover with chocolate sauce.

Crème Patisserie (Pastry Cream)
To fill cream puffs for Profiteroles
Yield: 2 cups

The secret of any custard is patience. The custard must not cook too quickly or it will burn and become lumpy. If the pastry cream becomes too thick when it cools, stir in a little heavy cream to smooth.

5 jumbo egg yolks
⅓ cup granulated sugar
⅛ teaspoon salt
3 ½ tablespoons cornstarch
2 cups whole milk

2 teaspoons vanilla extract
Optional: 1 ounce semi-sweet
chocolate for chocolate
pastry cream

1. Separate eggs, making sure no white membrane remains around the yolks. Reserve the whites for meringue cookies and set yolks aside.
2. Combine sugar, salt and cornstarch and sift into a bowl. Add 1/4 cup of the milk and stir to combine. Stir in remaining milk.

3. Strain the mixture into a saucepan.
4. Cook, stirring, over medium heat until mixture is hot. Stir 2 tablespoons of the hot mixture into the yolks before adding the yolks to the saucepan. Cook the mixture over medium heat, stirring constantly with a wooden spoon and smoothing with a wire whisk until thick. If mixture begins to stick to the bottom of the pan, reduce the heat immediately. (Chocolate may be added at this time) Stir in vanilla and remove from stove. Cover tightly with plastic film to cool.
5. Fill cream puffs (Pâte-À-Choux), or use between cake layers or under fresh fruit in pies, as the base for Trifle, or the best chocolate pudding ever!

Chocolate Sauce
Yield: 2 cups
Recipe can be doubled

1 cup heavy cream
2 tablespoons butter

10 ounces semi-sweet
  chocolate
1 teaspoon vanilla

1. Stir together the cream and butter in a small saucepan over low heat. When the butter melts, stir in the chocolate. Cook over low heat, stirring occasionally, until the chocolate melts into the cream mixture and becomes smooth. Stir in the vanilla to serve over the profiterole puffs.

"Chantons notre victoire, Vivre le son du canon."
(Let's sing our victory, Hurrah for the sound of the cannon.)
— La Carmagnole, 1792

The Revolution

On October 6, 1789, we heard a terrible noise outside the palace. Six thousand women preceded by ten drummers and four cannons were marching on Le Grand Trianon at Versailles armed with broom handles, pitchforks, swords, kitchen knives, skewers, and old pistols. There were also men disguised as women. They were wearing red hats and they were shouting, "Kill the Queen". We ran with the ladies in waiting and hid in the narrow secret chamber that separated the young Dauphin's bedroom from the King's. When the King was taken captive, Marie took us out of our hiding place to be with him. We were all arrested and taken in the royal coach to the Tuileries Palace outside Paris. It took seven hours to get to the magnificent royal residence that had been built for Catherine de Medici in 1564 outside Paris. The roads were lined with our French subjects who were brandishing weapons and shouting horrible things at us.

We were held prisoner in our own palace for several weeks. Then, one evening some friends of the king brought peasants' clothing for us to wear. We quickly changed into our disguises and tiptoed through the palace without candles in the middle of the night.

The Revolution

Outside, hidden in the thick of the trees, waited an old coach in which the common people traveled. We drove all night, almost one hundred sixty miles to the outskirts of the city of Varennes. Feeling safe, we climbed out of the coach. When the people saw us, they began to cheer and fall to their knees chanting, "Long live the King". *But then the police came and arrested us. They made us turn the coach around immediately to return to Paris. We were all so very tired we just did as they said. We rode back to the Tuileries where we were once again held captive.*

Then on August 10ᵗʰ, 1792, the revolutionaries stormed the Tuileries intending to kill us all. Madame Royale grabbed me under her arm and ran to the huge covered riding ring known as the royal equestrian academy that had been turned into an amphitheater where the National Constituent Assembly met. We hid in a dark cubby hole in the far corner where, horrified, we watched the angry crowd murdering the kind people who had been our guards. When we were found, we were taken to the Tower which was the state prison for convicted murderers and thieves. I did not understand why the people who captured us weren't brutal or rude. It was as though we were being escorted into a hotel instead of the prison we feared was our destiny of no return. It was very confusing to the children who heard the people outside screaming for our blood.

At first, Madame Royale hid me under her skirts, hoping I would not be discovered. What if they took

*me from her? What would she do without me? What
would I do without her? But, they didn't seem to notice
or care about the princess who could not ascend to the
throne or her cat that she would have protected with her
life. Their mission was to get rid of the hated King and
Queen and their son, the young Dauphin, who would
become King Louis XVII after his father's death.*

*Although Madame Royale was given enough food to
sustain her, it consisted mainly of watered down soup
with boiled beef and coarse bread. We played a little
game every night when they opened the locked door
and placed it before her. She sniffed appreciatively
and then happily announced that it was the special
onion soup her cook used to make that was infused
with the amazing Pinot Noir wine from Burgundy.
She carefully removed some of the beef to share with
me, but it was not necessary. Although pampered by
French royalty for over a hundred years, my heritage
from Turkey had surfaced. The good blood in my veins
surged to the excitement of survival. Every night
while my mistress slept, I sneaked through the small
open space of the locked door to explore the prison. I
found a banquet in every corridor. Tiny, succulent
field mice were everywhere, waiting to satisfy my
appetite. There were also large rats, but I did not
bother with them. Why should I hunt monsters when
delicate little morsels were so easily attainable?"*

She stopped talking to lick her lips in appreciation. I could
not imagine catching a live mouse, much less eating it raw
without garlic or cream sauce.

The Revolution

*Don't stop now, Hanako. What became of you and
Madame Royale? Were you sent to the guillotine
with the Queen?*

It took a few minutes for her to return to her past existence
in the prison. I knew that the worst was about to come.

*After they murdered the king, they separated us
from Queen Marie. Then they took her away in the
middle of the night to the Conciergerie, which was
the very worst of all the prisons in Paris. The year
was 1793. They gave her a mock trial where they
turned her answers to their rude questions around
so she would look guilty. One morning shortly after,
I heard trumpets and cheers and knew that Marie
was being taken to the guillotine to have her head
chopped off. I couldn't stay with Madame Royale. I
had to go to my Queen. I ran out of the cell, down
the long corridors and out into the streets of Paris.
Realizing that I might be recognized as the Royal
Chat, I sneaked into the alley and rolled in the wet
mud to conceal my fur. Looking like a street cat, I
hurried to the screaming crowds and took my place
directly below the scaffold of the guillotine. As the
cheers grew louder, I could see Marie in the distance.
Whereas Louis had been driven in a carriage, my
beautiful, beloved Queen was being transported
in a garbage cart. With her head erect, she seemed
not to notice anyone as the cart passed through the
throngs of her once adoring subjects. She was only
37 years old but her hair had turned pure white
and she looked like an old woman. Then, her eyes*

shifted in my direction. Oh, my God, she recognized me! A glint of a smile passed over her lips and her eyes filled with tears. I looked her straight in her face and silently promised that I would never leave her precious Madame Royale. I know she understood because she nodded her head ever so slightly in my direction. I turned and dashed between the legs of the mob, never stopping until I reached the jail apartment of my mistress. When she saw my filthy disguise, she grabbed me into her arms and held me close, sobbing until there were no more tears within her broken heart. From our prison we could hear the cheers of 'Vive la nation! Vive la République!

We had been imprisoned in the Tuilleries in 1789 and in that awful Tower for over a year. Madame Royale and I remained in our apartment alone. I was all she had left. The last of her possessions had been taken after they killed La Reine Marie Antoinette. One morning, two strange men came to ask her questions about her mother and father that were impossible to answer. They came the next day again and asked the same questions that were not questions at all but statements turned into questions vilifying the king and queen politically, socially and morally that justified their executions in order to save France and its peoples. She always answered that she knew nothing of her parents' affairs because she was only a child

They returned her candle and matchbox to give some light at night, and, they gave us soap and water to clean ourselves and a broom to sweep the floor. They also brought wood to make a fire, and some paper and ink but would not give her any books to read. She cried almost all the time because she knew that no one was taking care of her little brother in the cell upstairs.

Every day she wrote a lengthy description about her captors and her endless hours in prison with the rationed paper and ink they had provided. At night, when she was certain no one would come to her chamber, she would write a note to her brother telling him how much she loved him and that he must be very brave. Then she rolled up the paper and placed it firmly between my teeth.

"Mon petit chat, take this to the little King to read. Go quickly lest you are seen by the guards."

Slinking carefully past her guards, I crept stealthily along the damp walls and up the narrow stone steps to his small, dark prison room. The young king was always waiting for my arrival in anticipation of news about his family. When he saw me, the unhappy child's face lit up. He would hold me and kiss me and then remove the precious note from between my teeth. When I left, I would turn back to see him reading it over and over, cherishing the last link to his beloved family. After my dear Queen was murdered, the notes from his sister were the only hope he had left. They were hardly feeding him and he had become painfully thin and ghostly pale. The months without sunlight and sanitation were more than his little body could withstand.

One night when I went to his cell, the gentle ten year-old was lying still on his bug infested mattress. He was filthy and seemed to have a high fever. His legs were swollen and he was coughing. I jumped up and rubbed against him, meowing softly to tell him that his sister was all right and that he should be brave because we would all surely be spared now that the Queen was dead. But, he didn't understand. He no longer cared about anyone, not even himself. There was nothing I could do to help. When I went to his cell the next night, it was empty. They had taken him away. I returned to Madame Royale with her note still in my mouth. When she saw it, she held me in her arms and cried as if her heart would break. I cried also. The little king was dead.

We were sure each night would be our last. I curled up into her lap for her to hold me close with her head buried in my neck. And then, around two o'clock in the morning on a dreadfully cold night, the door to our cell opened. It was December 18, 1795. The wind was screaming outside during a terrible snow storm and we could not hear anything. We thought they had come to take us to our death. Instead, the guards gave her a heavy cape and told us to follow them. We were being released. The National Assembly had traded us for the freedom of a group of French Revolutionists that were imprisoned in Austria. Holding me tightly under her cape for protection and warmth, we boarded a coach that took us to Vienna where the Duc d'Angoulême was waiting to marry her. It was the day before her seventeenth birthday, seven of which she was imprisoned. I had lived almost my entire life in captivity, knowing freedom and comfort less than one year. But we loved each other and it was because of love that we survived. The remaining eight years of my life were spent in luxury as the favorite feline of Madame Royale's Executive Chef (Küchenchef) in a beautiful Austrian kitchen where I grew fat and lazy while I awaited my exiled French Princess and her Duc to return from their travels through Europe. I sampled Wiener Schnitzel with Spätzle, fluffy egg dumplings, and cabbage dishes made with apples, walnuts and sausages, or stuffed with rice and pork from the Serbians while it was being prepared for her distinguished guests. Then there was a warm Apple Strudel, and a light pudding made with rice and raisins and a cake that had six layers called Doboschtorte. Although most cats do not like sweets, I was a French cat born to luxury and excess.

I was trying to remember all the details of her story when she began again.

Would you like me to tell you about my next life when I was reborn in France in the 19th century? I was one of the first Angoras imported to America. It was because of me that all white cats became known as Angoras.

127

It was time to grab the ball and run with it.

No, thank you. Although I am impressed with your royal French blood, I can see without taxing my imagination that you are no longer a pure Turkish Angora, or even a later breed of the Angora, but a mixture of many non-pedigreed felines that just happened to produce a throwback to a better lineage.

She hissed through her teeth. I decided it was time to depart. I jumped to the floor from Susan's bed and scampered out the door into the kitchen only a second before the sharp claws of her raised paw shot out to annihilate my pretty little pink nose.

Marie's Last Supper
Pâté to Lose One's Head Over
Yield: Approximately 2 cups

Make at least 24 hours before serving for the flavors to settle. This pâté may be served in the crock accompanied by crackers or spread on toast points and heated.

3 duck livers
¼ pound chicken livers
4 tablespoons butter
1 large shallot, peeled and
 sliced thin
1 clove garlic, peeled and
 sliced thin

1-inch piece ginger, peeled
 and sliced thin
¼ pound white mushrooms,
 sliced thin
½ cup cooked duck meat
1 tablespoon cream sherry
¼ cup chardonnay wine
1 tablespoon brandy

2 hard-boiled jumbo eggs
⅛ scant teaspoon cloves
⅛ teaspoon nutmeg
Salt and pepper to taste

Optional: Black truffle
pieces or small black olives
sliced very thin to decorate
the top

1. Wash the livers, removing any connective tissue.
2. In a deep skillet, melt the butter and sauté the shallot, garlic, ginger, and mushrooms over very low heat until limp. Add the livers and continue to cook, turning them over often to cook on all sides.
3. Increase the heat to medium-high and add the sherry, wine, and brandy. Bring to a quick boil. Remove the skillet from the heat. Cool to room temperature.
4. Pulverize or purée in a food processor, adding just enough of the gravy from the pan to incorporate the mixture. Do not add too much or pâté will be "soupy".
5. Add the hard-boiled egg yolks, cloves, and nutmeg and blend again. Taste for salt and pepper. Optional: Stir in the truffle pieces.
6. Fill a crock, cover, and refrigerate 24 hours or longer before serving.
7. Optional: Decorate the top with thinly sliced black olives.

Tower Gruel Fantasy
Madame Royale's Onion Soup
Yield: 6-8 servings

2 tablespoons butter or butter substitute
2 tablespoons olive oil
1 clove finely minced garlic
6 medium to large yellow or white onions, sliced thin on the round
1 tablespoon granulated sugar
¼ cup Pinot Noir wine
3 tablespoons brandy or cognac
3 tablespoons all-purpose flour

5 cups strong homemade beef stock or concentrated canned consommé
1 cup water
2 tablespoons tomato ketchup
Salt to taste
½ teaspoon black pepper, or to taste
6 thick slices French bread, toasted on one side
Gruyère or Fontina cheese, crumbled or sliced thin
Parmesan cheese, grated

1. Heat the butter and olive oil in a soup pot. Add the garlic and onions. Stir in the sugar to help brown the onions. Stir in the wine and brandy. Cook together until the onions are very soft and lightly colored.
2. Stir in the flour. Stir in the beef stock, a little at a time, bringing the soup to a boil. Stir in the ketchup. Lower the heat and cook approximately 10 minutes.
3. Taste for salt and pepper.
4. Toast the bread on one side.
5. Ladle the soup into ovenproof bowls. Set the bread on top, toast side into the soup.
6. Set the cheese on top. Place under the broiler until bubbly. Sprinkle with Parmesan. Serve immediately.

And, oh, yes, you may warm canned fried onions strings to sprinkle over the top of the soup.

Free at Last
Viennese Wienerschnitzel
Yield: 4 servings

Chicken or pork can be exchanged for veal.
The addition of oil in the egg holds the breading in place and ensures a crisp result.

4 scaloppini of veal, cut thin from the leg	1 cup fine dry toasted bread crumbs
Sprinkling of salt and pepper	1 tablespoon butter (or lard)
¾ cup all-purpose flour	1 tablespoon vegetable
1 jumbo egg, lightly beaten	shortening
1 tablespoon salad oil	

1. Sprinkle salt and pepper lightly over the veal or chicken. If pork is substituted, brush with lemon juice before breading.
2. Measure the flour onto a plate or sheet of waxed paper.
3. Measure the breadcrumbs onto a plate or sheet of waxed paper.
4. Beat the egg in a wide bowl. Mix in the oil.
5. Dip the cutlets into the flour, turning to cover both sides. Shake off excess flour.
6. Dip the cutlets in the egg to cover.
7. Shake off excess egg and dip the cutlets into the crumbs, covering both sides heavily.
8. Set the cutlets on wax paper for 30 minutes.

9. Heat the butter and oil in a large skillet. When it is very hot, fry the schnitzel to golden brown on both sides. It will cook quickly. Do not allow the fat to burn. Do not overcook. Turn just one time.

Note: Schnitzel should never be served dry. It should almost be swimming in the fat.

Set lemon slices on top to serve and sprinkle capers over. Anchovy filets are also a popular topping. When it is topped with a fried egg, it becomes Schnitzel à la Holstein. Accompany with Spätzle or Fluffy Egg Dumplings.

Spätzle
Yield: 4 servings. Recipe can be doubled

1 cup plus 2 tablespoons
  sifted all-purpose flour
½ teaspoon salt
Sprinkling of black pepper
1 jumbo egg, beaten

⅓ cup water
Pot of boiling water with 1
  teaspoon salt
4 tablespoons butter

1. Add salt to the flour. Add egg with a fork. Stir to combine. Stir in water slowly. When the batter is stiff but combined and smooth, remove it to a floured surface.
2. Press the dough flat on the floured surface.
3. Bring the pot of water to a boil. Scrape small pieces of the dough off and drop into the boiling water. Boil gently 8-10 minutes. (Remove and taste to make sure they are cooked through)
4. Turn pot over through a colander. Toss the spätzle in the colander to remove all moisture.

5. Melt butter in another pot and toss in the spätzle. Taste for salt and pepper. Serve with the Schnitzel.
Note: Parmesan cheese may also be sprinkled over them but it must be freshly grated.

Fluffy Egg Dumplings
Yield: Approximately 6 dumplings

1 cup all-purpose sifted flour
1 level tablespoon baking powder
¼ teaspoon salt

Tiny pinch white pepper
1 jumbo egg
½ cup whole milk
3-4 cups chicken broth

1. Combine the flour, baking powder, salt and white pepper.
2. Beat the egg with a fork. Stir in the milk. Stir in the flour mixture. The batter should be very stiff. Allow it to sit 15 minutes or longer. Stir again.
3. Bring the broth to a gentle boil in a wide mouth pot. Dip a soup spoon into the broth before filling it with the batter. Dip the spoon into the broth with the batter. Continue to drop batter slowly, making sure the dumplings do not touch each other.
4. Cover the pot, leaving the lid on a tilt for steam to escape. Simmer 10 minutes. Serve immediately.

Austrian Cabbage with Apple and Walnuts
Yield: Approximately 6 servings

2 pounds red or white
or Savoy cabbage or a
combination
1 large onion
½ teaspoon coarse sea salt
2 tablespoons walnut or
olive oil
½ cup apple juice

¼ cup apple cider vinegar
2 pounds Fuji, Ambrosia or
Gala apples, peeled and cut
into small pieces
¼ cup dark brown sugar
1 teaspoon ground sage
½ cup broken walnuts
Salt to taste

1. Slice the cabbage in half. Cut out and discard the core. Chop into irregular small pieces with a knife, not in the food processor.
2. Peel the onion. Cut it in half. Slice into thin circles on the round. Cut the circles in half.
3. Combine the cabbage and onion in a deep skillet with the salt and oil. Cook slowly over low heat, covered, until the cabbage is soft.
4. Stir in the apples, apple cider vinegar and sugar. Stir in the sage. Continue to cook over low heat until very soft, stirring frequently. This will take approximately 45 minutes.
5. Stir in the walnuts.
6. Remove from the heat and let it rest in the covered skillet for 15 minutes.
   Taste for salt and pepper to serve.
   Note: Cooked sausage of choice can be added with the apples. Cook in advance. Drain off the fat and crumble. Do not add sage if the sausage has it in its ingredients.

Stuffed Cabbage Austrian-Serb
Approximately 8 rolls

1 cup white rice
2 cups water
1 onion
1 ½ pounds lean ground beef
½ teaspoon salt
¼ teaspoon black pepper
1 large green cabbage
2 – 14 ½ ounce cans diced
tomatoes, plain or seasoned
6 ounces tomato paste

1 tablespoon plus 1 teaspoon
sour salt (citric acid)
1 clove crushed garlic
½ cup firmly-packed dark
brown sugar
1 ½ teaspoons minced fresh
ginger or ¾ teaspoon
ground
2 bay leaves

1. Bring rice and water to a boil, stirring. Reduce heat to low and continue cooking, uncovered, until water has absorbed.
2. Mince onion (food processor). Stir into cooked rice. Mix with beef, salt and pepper.
3. Remove cabbage leaves carefully from head. If leaves will not come away without breaking, cut out one inch of the center core and set cabbage core side down into 2 inches boiling water for a minute or two. When leaves pull away easily, pull them off, one at a time.
4. Combine canned tomatoes, tomato paste, sour salt, garlic, brown sugar and ginger in a shallow baking dish.
5. Prepare cabbage rolls: The inside leaves are smaller and lighter in color. Wrap the beef mixture in them first and then cover each with a larger green leaf. Set approximately two large spoonsful of the beef mixture in the center of each cabbage leaf. Fold flaps over. Set leaf, flap-side down, in a larger green leaf and fold flaps over to create rolls. Set

flap-side down in sauce. Cook or refrigerate to cook later in the day.

6. Preheat oven to 350°F. Spoon sauce over cabbage rolls. Cover dish with foil. Bake 30 minutes.

Apple Strudel (Apfelstrudel)
Yield: 2 strudel, 6 pieces each

Do not allow filo pastry sheets to reach room temperature or they will become unmanageable and break apart.

4 large Granny Smith apples, peeled, cored, sliced thin
1 cup granulated sugar
1 teaspoon cinnamon
¼ teaspoon nutmeg
1 cup dried cranberries or golden raisins

Optional: 1 cup pecan pieces
1 package filo (phyllo) pastry sheets, defrosted to cold stage
¼ pound unsalted butter or butter substitute, melted
½ cup corn flake crumbs

1. Preheat oven to 350°F.
2. Peel, core and slice the apples. Combine sugar, cinnamon and nutmeg. Toss with the apples. Stir in the cranberries (raisins). Stir in the nuts.
3. Defrost filo pastry to the cold stage. Do not allow it to become warm or it will fall apart when handling.
4. Melt the butter. Separate 2 sheets and place them on a clean dish towel. Brush butter over the entire area of the sheets. Sprinkle corn flake crumbs over lightly.
5. Place another 2 layers on top. Brush with butter. Sprinkle corn flake crumbs over lightly. Repeat. Repeat again but do not brush with butter and do not sprinkle with crumbs.

6. Spoon apple filling along the long side of the dough, approximately 2 inches from the edge. Brush the edge with butter. Roll dough up with the towel to cover the filling. (This will hold the dough together. As you roll, release the towel and brush with butter. Turn the log over and brush again. Carefully set on a baking sheet covered with parchment paper.
7. Score the log lightly with a sharp knife to mark the portions. You should have 6-8 pieces per log.
8. Set into the oven and bake approximately 40 minutes, or until golden and flaky.
   Note: This may be reheated at 300°F or set into a warming oven. Do not slice until ready to serve. Accompany with vanilla ice cream.

Rice Pudding (Reisauflauf)
Yield: Approximately 6 servings
Recipe can be doubled

¼ cup long-grain white rice
½ cup water
Pinch of salt
2 jumbo eggs
½ cup granulated sugar
2 teaspoons vanilla extract
2 scant cups whole milk
   (Lactose intolerant:
Exchange Lactaid or
Almond milk)
¼ cup golden raisins or dried
   cranberries
Deep casserole dish
Sprinkling of grated nutmeg
   for the top (freshly grated is
   best)

1. Preheat oven to 375°F.
2. Bring water with a pinch of salt to a boil. Stir in rice. Reduce heat to medium. Boil, uncovered, 10 minutes. Do

not stir. Cover. Reduce heat to simmer. Cook until water is absorbed and rice is tender, approximately 15-20 minutes longer. You will have one cup cooked rice.

3. Beat eggs, sugar and vanilla with a wire whisk or hand electric beater. Whisk in the milk in a slow, steady stream.
4. Spoon as much rice as you like along the bottom of the casserole dish. Mix the raisins (cranberries) with the rice, making sure entire bottom has equal amount.
5. Pour in the pudding. (If, for some reason, the eggs have not incorporated correctly and you see streaks of yolk, pour the mixture through a strainer)
6. Grate the nutmeg over the top.
7. Place the dish into a pan of water to reach one-third up the sides.
8. Place on an oven rack one-third from the bottom. Bake 55-60 minutes or until set and a knife inserted in the center comes out 'clean'. Remove pudding from the water immediately or it will continue to cook.
9. Refrigerate several hours or overnight.

Doboschtorte
Yield: 5-6 layers

4 jumbo graded egg yolks
2 whole jumbo graded whole
  eggs
½ cup granulated sugar
½ teaspoon fresh orange juice
1 teaspoon vanilla
½ cup all-purpose flour,
  sifted 2 times

4 jumbo graded egg whites
½ teaspoon cr. of tartar
1 tablespoon granulated sugar
9 or 10 inch cake pan
6 rounds of parchment paper
  cut to fit the bottom of
  the pan

1. Preheat oven to 350°F.
2. Allow the eggs to come to room temperature.
3. Separate 4 eggs, with the yolks in one large crockery bowl and the whites in a second bowl. Set aside the bowl with the egg whites to a warm place.
4. Add the two whole eggs to the bowl with the egg yolks.
5. Add the sugar, orange juice and vanilla and set the bowl over simmering water. Beat on the highest speed of a hand electric mixer until very thick, white and mousse-like. This will take at least 10 minutes. Remove from the heat and stir in the flour with a spatula. Do not beat it in or you will lose volume.
6. Beat the egg whites on the highest speed of an electric mixer until foamy. Add the cream of tartar and continue beating until very thick. Add the sugar and beat for a few seconds until smooth.
7. Fold the whites into the yolk mixture.
8. Grease the bottom of the cake pan with a little oil to hold the parchment paper in place.

9. Spoon a very thin layer of the batter to cover the bottom of the pan, leaving a quarter inch space around the edge.
10. Set on a rack in the oven ⅓ from the bottom. Bake no longer than 10 minutes, or until light brown.
11. Turn the pan upside down onto wax or parchment paper on a flat surface. Peel the parchment paper off from the bottom immediately.
12. Repeat the procedure to bake until all the batter is used. You will have enough batter to create 5-6 layers.

"Let the Looking-glass creatures, whatever they be,
Come and dine with the Red Queen, the White Queen and me!"
— Lewis Carroll, Through the Looking Glass, 1868

Sakie's Adventure
in Wonderland

HE DIDN'T NOTICE ME ON the other side of the screen door. I had never seen a cat such as him. His lustrous coat that shimmered in the afternoon sun was uncanny. One minute I saw brown and red stripes, and the next minute the stripes changed to pink and purple. His head was wider than his body and he was smiling. He was having his own party with one of the bananas that had fallen from the tree at the back of our house overlooking Miami's Biscayne Bay. As he pounced on one end, the other sprang upward in flight. When it landed he jumped at it again. It bounced to his right. He leapt. It took off to his left. I braced my weight on my back legs and scratched at the screen. He shifted his attention to my direction.

Meow, I said, and sat, raising my paw in my signature Bobtail greeting.

Meow, he answered, and strode over to the porch to get a closer look.

I'm Sakie. I live here. What kind of cat are you?

Don't you recognize me? I am the Cheshire Cat.

Of course, "The Gingham dog and the Cheshire cat, side by side on the table sat......"

No, no, that was the Calico Cat in the poem by Eugene Field. I am the famous Cheshire cat from Alice in Wonderland by Lewis Carroll. Can't you see my grin?

It was impossible to miss it. All I could see was a mouth filled with white teeth. They were all exactly the same size. He didn't have any sharp incisors like other cats. The mouth took up his whole face with the exception of huge round eyes that stared out at me.

I'm so sorry. What is Wonderland and who is Alice?

Wonderland was the home of my ancestors. Alice was the little girl who went through the looking glass.

What is a looking glass?

That's what humans once called the mirror.

So, what happened to her?

When she reached the other side of the mirror, she found herself in a strange land inhabited by creatures and people unlike any in your world. There was the Queen of Hearts and a weird rabbit and the Mad Hatter, and yours truly, the Cheshire Cat.

Oh, how I would like to chase a real rabbit, I confessed. *Have you ever gone back?*

Never, but I guess with a bit of magical wishing, it might be possible.

My heart began to pound in anticipation.

May I come with you? I can wish very hard and I dream magical thoughts. I could help it happen.

I don't know. The tales of Wonderland have been passed down through fourteen generations of my family, but no Cheshire cat has ever returned.

There's a double mirror – looking glass – on mom's dresser. Wait here while I fetch it.

I scampered as fast as my paws could go into *mom* and *dad's* bedroom and jumped up to the dresser. Getting behind the mirror, I nosed it to the edge. As it tumbled to the floor, I prayed it would not break. Protected by its metal binding, it rolled to a halt at the base of the dresser. Turning my body sideways, I slowly pushed it across the carpet until it reached the tile floor in the hall. Once it was on the slippery tile, I nosed and pawed it easily toward the screen door. The magnification side of the mirror faced me, reflecting an illusion of a cat's head three times mine.

Does it matter if the mirror reflects us in different sizes, I asked, with a worried meow.

I don't think so. A mirror is a mirror. Ok, now, you have to concentrate on jumping through it at the same moment as I.

Why are we jumping through it? Suppose it breaks.
Mom will be really angry.

It's the only way we can get to Wonderland, my new
friend. You're the one who wanted to go, so you will
have to take a chance.

But, suppose we can't come back?
That's another chance we'll be taking.

I held my breath for an instant. I knew I was being foolish, even foolhardy, but Wonderland was too appealing an adventure to forego and this would certainly be my only opportunity. The Cheshire looked impatient.

When I finish my chant, think Magic. Count to
three and jump.

He stood in a pouncing position, bowed his head and began to chant. His tail swished with such force that the little leaves around him scattered to safety.

Great mirror of magic
As we see through you.
Great mirror of magic
We know what you can do.
Great mirror of dreams
Listen to our miew.
Mirror of our dreams
Let us come through.

I counted to three and leapt at my reflection. I felt my body catch up into a wind that had me spinning as though in a tornado. Then I sailed through a huge empty space until I landed feet first onto a pillow-soft ground.

Cheshire, Cheshire, where are you?

When my senses kicked in, I realized that I was standing in a field of catnip that reached to the top of my ears. The perfume of this aphrodisiac enveloped me and I fell onto my back and rolled around in its glorious scent. Then I saw the tiny white mice. Thousands of succulent tidbits played tag with each other under the plants. I stood and worked my way through the thick foliage toward a light in the distance and found myself on a path flanked with fluffy yarn and millions of beanie balls and kitten toys tied with string. Mounds of cooked shrimp were piled on platters, and finely chopped cooked ham filled gigantic bowls.

Oh Great Mother of cats, where am I?

Something or somebody whizzed by, wearing an oversized top hat that looked like the one Dr. Seuss had drawn in "The Cat in the Hat". It was also wearing a bow tie that stretched from one shoulder to the other if, in fact, they were shoulders, and it was carrying a tray filled with clattering teacups. Right on its heels was a gigantic rabbit wearing a similar bow tie and carrying a tray filled with tiny cakes.

Stop, I said, please stop! Who are you? Where are you going? And, where is the Cheshire Cat?

The rabbit slid to a stop, causing some of the cakes fly off the tray.

I'm the March Hare, and I'm trying to keep up with the Mad Hatter for our tea party with Alice. Now, pick up the cakes before the Queen sees they're on the ground or she'll have my head.

Oh my, then Alice really is here. May I join you?

Are you mad?

No, I'm Sakie.

I mean, you could join us if you were mad like us.

I'm not angry at anything.

Mad as in crazy. We're all crazy here, you know.

The Cheshire cat isn't crazy.

Oh, yes I am. Otherwise I would not be here.

I looked in the direction of the voice. Sitting on top of a pile of cooked shrimp was his mouth; nothing else of him, just his mouth, grinning. I started to say something, but he disappeared.

We're late for the tea party, the Rabbit said hurriedly. *Are you coming or not?*

I scooped up the cakes from the ground and scampered after him into a thick forest. Almost immediately there was an opening with a table filled with teacups and cakes and butter and jam. And, Alice was sitting at the head seat, her hands primly placed on her lap. She was very pretty with a blue bow tied in her long hair, but she was no taller than I.

Are you really Alice? And why are you so small?

"I shrank when I ate a cake. Here, have a taste."
I took a bite. It was delicious. It tasted like tuna fish. I took another but, instead of shrinking, I felt myself growing taller, so taller that I was at eye level with the tops of the trees and could barely see the Rabbit and Hatter and Alice at my feet.

Oh my, said the Hatter. *Take another bite before you trample us all to death.*

As soon as I swallowed the last bite, I felt myself shrinking back to normal.

Alice jammed a whole slice of cake into her mouth and pushed herself away from the table.

"I'm finished. We shall go into the Queen's garden now. But, Sakie, let me warn you. You have been stealing my characters since Cheshire brought you here. If the Queen finds out that you've taken Lewis Carroll's story and written it as your own, she will have you beheaded immediately."

I could see she was growing taller. In the instant it took us to reach the huge white trellis that led into the garden, she had become the size of a real girl.

Sakie's Adventure in Wonderland

I'm sorry, but how else can I describe Wonderland?
It's not my fault I didn't invent it.

I was about to become depressed when I saw rows of giant playing cards. They were decorated with clubs and spades and diamonds. The most beautiful had bright red hearts painted on them. And, they all had numbers printed on each of their four corners. There were hundreds of them, all bustling around to get into a sort of military formation. Then I saw what the excitement was about. The King and Queen of Hearts were at the back of a procession of cards with faces on them. And, they were moving in my direction. In an instant they were in front of me.

What are you? The Queen shouted.

I'm Sakie Cat.

A white cat? There is no such thing as a white cat in
Wonderland. We have white rabbits and white mice
but no white cats. Leave my kingdom this instant
or I shall have you beheaded!

"She can't do that", whispered Alice. "She's only a card."

That's ok for you to say. You're the same size as her,
but I'm small enough for her to whack my head off
my neck with the sharp corner of one of those other
cards."

"You do have a point", pondered Alice. "Perhaps you should make a run for it."

I really want to go home, but I don't know which way to run. The Cheshire cat brought me here and disappeared. He's only come back once, and then it was only his mouth.

Don't be silly, you fretful cat, I've been right next to you the entire time.

And, sure enough, all of him was sitting on Alice's shoulder, his big teeth grinning from ear to ear.

All you have to do is think about the mirror. Imagine you're looking into it, count to three and jump! You'll be home in a jiffy. And then, there was an empty space on Alice's shoulder.

I closed my eyes and counted to three. My head and entire body began to spin uncontrollably. I heard a loud thump and awakened to find that I was back on the porch inside the screen door. I ran into the hall, giddy with relief.

Sam, Sam, I'm back. I found the looking glass and came through. I'm home.

What do you mean, 'back'? Back from where? You've been sound asleep by the screen door the entire afternoon.

No I haven't. I've been with the Cheshire cat in Wonderland. There were toys and balls and yarn and miles of fields filled with cat nip. I saw Alice and the March Hare and had tea with the Mad

Hatter and almost had my head chopped off by the Queen of Hearts

Did you say you were with the Cheshire Cat?

Yes, it was his magic that took us through the looking glass.

Sakie, there is no such animal as the Cheshire Cat. The Cheshire cat is an imaginary character of Lewis Carroll's. And, for your information, Alice did not get to Wonderland by jumping through any mirror. She crawled into a rabbit hole in the earth to follow a pink-eyed white rabbit that had a watch in his waist-coat pocket and fell down the well into wonderland. It was in the story, "Through the Looking Glass," that she crawled through a mirror. If you're going to dream, at least get your books in order.

That's not true. He was right outside, playing with a banana that had fallen from the tree. I mewed to him and he told me his ancestors were in Wonderland and, if we wished really hard, we could jump into a mirror just like Alice. I pushed mom's mirror to the door and he chanted magic and we counted to three and jumped. Oh, Sam, it was so wonderful, but also scary because I wanted to go home but didn't know how to find my way back.

Now you're confused with Dorothy in "The Wizard of Oz". Honestly Sakie, sometimes you're really

151

impossible because you can't tell fantasy from reality when you dream. I'm going outside and, when I come back, I do not want to hear one more word about Wonderland.

I curled into a ball and sulked.

Fifteen minutes later he returned, carrying an oversized playing card in his mouth. On it was a picture of the Queen of Hearts. When *mom* opened the door for him, she noticed something shining on the outside porch.

"My mirror", she exclaimed. "How did my mirror get out here?"

Wonderland Tea Sandwiches

Smoked Salmon on Buttered Bread:
Yield: 36 open-faced sandwiches

These sandwiches are most appealing with
fresh tarragon or tiny fresh tarragon flowers to
decorate the top. Tarragon is easy to grow.

1 pound Scotch or
  Norwegian smoked salmon,
  pre-sliced
¼ pound unsalted butter
18 slices whole grain bread,
  thinly sliced and cut into
  rectangles
6 ounces tiny capers

1 cup finely-chopped mild
  onion
1bunche minced fresh dill or
  tarragon
1 lemon cut into wedges
Dill or tarragon sprigs for
  decoration

1. Cut salmon to fit each piece of bread. If slices overlap, fold the ends underneath. Lightly butter the bread. Combine the capers, onion and dill or tarragon and press a bit into the butter. Place a slice of salmon on top.
2. Decorate with finely chopped tarragon, dill or parsley. Serve on a glass platter with lemon wedges.

Cucumber

1 large English (seedless) cucumber, unpeeled	A loaf of sliced soft white bread, crusts removed
8 ounces cream cheese	4 tablespoons softened butter
½ cup minced scallion greens	A bunch of watercress with
½ cup minced watercress	stems
Salt and a touch of white pepper to taste	

1. Slice the cucumber and set the slices into a colander to drain off any excess water for 30 minutes. Chop fine with a chef's knife, not in a food processor.
2. Combine the cucumber, cream cheese, minced scallions and watercress. Refrigerate several hours or overnight.
3. Remove the crusts from the bread and roll each slice slightly with a rolling pin. Do not roll thin.
4. Lightly spread the softened butter across two edges of the bread slices. Spoon the cucumber mixture across the center of each piece and roll, using the buttered ends to "glue" the rolls.
5. Insert a sprig of watercress into the open end for decoration.

Directions for Pinwheel Sandwiches:

1. Purchase large loaves of soft white bread.
2. Cut away outer crusts of bread, saving them for crumbs or cheese sticks or bread pudding.
3. Slice lengthwise as thin as possible. Each loaf should yield 3-4 slices. Flatten the slices very slightly with a rolling pin.
4. Combine ingredients and spread a thin layer across each slice. Roll up tightly lengthwise from narrow end to narrow end. Wrap in wax paper or plastic wrap. Refrigerate until cold or overnight.
5. Slice the bread one-half inch thick and set on platters open side up. Top each pinwheel with a thin slice of sweet gherkins or pimento olives or sprig of parsley or cilantro. Garnish with cherry tomatoes, watercress or parsley.

Ham Salad
Yield: Approximately 40 Pinwheels

2 pounds cooked smoked ham	Mayonnaise to bind
½ cup sweet pickle relish	2 - 1 pound loaves unsliced bread

Place ham into the container of a food processor and mince. Add pickle relish and mince again. You will need very little mayonnaise to bind this mixture, so add it 1 tablespoon at a time.

Chicken Salad Pinwheels
Yield: Approximately 40 pinwheels

2 pounds chicken breasts, boned and skinned

1 teaspoon kosher salt

4 celery ribs, cut up

2 cups or more mayonnaise to bind

Salt and pepper to taste

2 - 1 pound loaves unsliced white bread

1. Cover breasts with water in a deep skillet. Add salt and bring to a boil. Reduce heat to medium-high and poach, covered, 20 minutes or longer, depending on their size. Chicken is done when there is no sign of opaque coloring when cut into. Cool and chop into tiny pieces or pulverize in a food processor.
2. Mince celery in a food processor and drain in a strainer at least 15 minutes. Add to chicken with enough mayonnaise to bind. Season with salt and pepper to taste.
3. Cut away the crust from the loaf. With a sharp serrated knife, cut the loaf into thin slices lengthwise. Flatten each slightly with a rolling pin to create uniform slices.
4. Spread chicken mixture over in a thin layer.
5. Roll up tightly. If the bread is wide, roll lengthwise. If it is narrow, roll up from end to end. Set each roll on wax paper and cover tightly. Refrigerate several hours or overnight.
6. Directly before serving, slice into pinwheels. Set open side up on platters and decorate each with sliced olives or sweet pickles.

"The mathematical probability of a common cat doing exactly as it pleases is the one scientific absolute in the world."
— Lynn M. Osband

Dark Places

I'T'S NOT MY FAULT I like to crawl into dark places. That's what I do. That's what cats have always done. We see a closet or cupboard or crevice and it compels us to enter. I also love high places. In fact, the higher I can climb the happier I am. This is probably due to my instinct that tells me high places are safe from other animals that can chase but do not know how to climb. Our art of climbing can get us into trouble as well. Sometimes we climb all the way to the top and then are afraid to come down. We know by instinct that we cannot come down a tree trunk the same way we crawled up. We do not have the same grip to hold on. Moving downward front paws first could cause us to skid and topple all the way to the bottom. And, we know if we jump from a branch or roof or even the top of a high piece of furniture, we could be seriously injured. So we stay where we have found ourselves until someone finds us.

My favorite high place was the top of the English breakfront in the dining room. In my youth I made it in three leaps. First the chair, second the sideboard, and finally with the grace and skill of the rare Andean cat of South America, I could fly all the way to the top. I knew I could have lived in the mountains at 10,000 feet with this elusive endangered wild cat, if given the opportunity. The first time I reached this extraordinary height, I could not figure out how to get back down. When the family found me sitting proudly with my head almost touching the nine-foot ceiling, they had to get out a ladder and crawl up to retrieve me. The next time they coaxed me down, cheering as I carefully maneuvered my way back to earth. Then, I mastered the procedure all by myself. Down I flew to the sideboard. Down I jumped to the chair. Down again I leaped to the soft carpet. What a superb cat I was! How I wish I could return to those glorious days!

Dark places were another story. I have been trapped a zillion times, causing the family to spend hours searching for me.

Kitchen cabinets and linen closets offered the most intrigue. Woe to the one who left a door opened to gather a pot or pan. I would wait for a moment and then, lickety-split, as soon as they looked in another direction, I would tip toe in, curling up in the darkest corner. Sometimes they didn't find me for hours, calling my name and opening every door except the one I was behind. I never made a sound. Why should I? If they were having a clever-cat day, they would figure out where I was by themselves. Sometimes I let them know where I was and conceded that they had won the game. But this was only when my tummy time clock went off when I became hungry, which I must admit was most of the day.

Only once did I cry to get out of a hiding place because of fear. Actually it was worse than fear. It was pure panic.

One morning when *dad* opened his sock drawer, I jumped in. All those rolled up socks were almost as soft as my Susan's hair and I cuddled into them just as he closed the drawer. Then he closed the closet door leaving me in complete darkness. Two hours passed. Another hour went by. I was hot and it was becoming difficult to breathe. Everyone was gone. I yowled as loudly as I could. I continued to yowl until my voice became too weak and I could only make a soft meowing sound.

Help, Help, I cried, *I'm suffocating.*

My tummy began to turn over and I became sick from

158

both ends all over his socks, many of which still had price tags attached.

Then I heard them enter the bedroom. I had lost so much strength that I could not meow, I could only whimper. *Dad* went into the closet to get his jacket.

"I smell something."

Mom came in and took a whiff.

"So do I."

I whimpered again. They finally heard me and opened the drawer. I looked up at them, and they looked down at me and the disgusting mess that had once been dad's favorite socks. Two big buckets were brought into the room. I was gingerly picked up and deposited in one. The socks were shoveled into the other. I was carried to the laundry room in the garage where I was dumped into the mop sink. *Mom* soaped me up and rinsed me three times with her most fragrant-smelling shampoo. Then she towel dried my fur and carried me back to the house. It wasn't until the next day that all the socks were washed, dried, and returned to a clean drawer. I never jumped into a drawer again. I had learned my lesson.

"A cat has absolute emotional honesty; human beings, for one reason or another, may hide their feelings, but a cat does not."
— Ernest Hemingway

Electric

SHE WAS LESS THAN A year old when she appeared
at the rectory behind our church. Her long hair fell in black
and tan blotches almost to the ground and her face was sort
of pushed in with a snub nose that could have belonged to a
Pekinese dog. Her tail was huge with thick fur and, when she
was content, it wagged instead of swishing like most cat tails.

Reverend James endeared himself to the children every
October 4th when he blessed the animals on St. Francis of Assisi
Day. When it became evident that she was going to be our
resident church cat, he baptized her. Oh, I don't mean he actually
baptized her but he did say in front of the neighborhood children,

"I give you the name, Abigail, the Hebrew name that means
Father of exaltation. It was the name of King David's third wife
who was described as *good in discretion*."

On weekdays she contentedly slept on the front porch
and watched the little lizards and squirrels at play. But every
Sunday, just as Rev. James began his sermon, Abigail would
appear at the narthex at the very back of the church. As she
deliberately made her way past the pews towards the altar, the
attention of every parishioner was diverted sideways. Visiting
tourists gasped and the regulars, who had come to expect the
performance, giggled. Not one to be upstaged by an amateur
feline, the good reverend always announced,

"If our visitor will please take a seat I will continue."

Abigail, as though on cue from a circus maestro, proceeded

up the steps and settled herself under the communion table where she peacefully slept until the end of the service.

One day she disappeared and, although everyone searched the neighborhood, she was seemingly gone. Three weeks later she strode back to the rectory carrying a kitten in her mouth. She dropped it under the porch and left. A half hour later she returned with another and another and another, until there were four.

As they grew larger it was evident they did not resemble her at all. They looked like American Tabbies except for an unusual anomaly. The feet of all four sported six toes that cat breeders call "polydactylism" that we in Florida refer to as "Hemingway cats" because of the six-toed cats owned by the late novelist, Ernest Hemingway, who lived in Key West.

Our reverend's wife gave each a Biblical name. The first was Joshua after Moses' successor, Joshua, who led the people across the Jordan River. The second was named Job who possessed a perfect character and never sinned. The third was Ezra who brought the Jewish exiles back to Jerusalem. The fourth and most beautiful became Gabriel, the only angel that could speak both Syriac and Chaldee, whom God sent as His messenger to Nazareth to bring the good news.

The kittens soon grew into large, muscular cats. They kept the church grounds free from mice but did not join mama for Sunday services.

Eight years went by and our dear reverend retired. The Search Committee worked long and hard to find a replacement. When it was finally announced that we would have a new minister, everyone buzzed with excitement and pitched in to make the house welcome for his arrival.

His first order of business was to inform the vestry that his wife was allergic to cats and if, no one in the congregation took them within the following week, he would call the Humane Society to pick them up for adoption. We all knew that most people do not adopt eight year-old cats, particularly those that have never lived in-doors, and old loyal Abigail, who had been bound to the congregation with allegiance and dependency, moved more slowly each day on arthritic legs. Their ultimate, if not intended, fate had just been determined.

We borrowed two cages with trap doors from my veterinarian. Bowls were filled with tuna and cat nip and placed inside. We parked down the street from the church and waited until there was no one around before hiding them in the bushes. It wasn't long before Abigail entered one and Ezra the other. We grabbed the cages and drove them home to our island, dropping Ezra in our front yard with water and food before bringing Abigail into the house. Then we took the cages back to the church and placed the same delicious enticement inside. When we returned the next morning we found Joshua and Job in the same cage and Gabriel in the other. Next to Gabriel was a strange creature that looked something like Abigail.

Who are you, I asked? The kitten answered with a distinctive chirping trill instead of a meow. We knew if we opened the cage to let it free, Gabriel would bolt also and, being one smart angel, she would not go into our trap a second time. Besides, if this funny-looking animal hung around the church, it would be bound for the Humane Society. It was easy to speculate that it might have been brought by a real angel for us to take care of. We resigned ourselves to a future of feeding four Hemingway and adopting the old cast-off and young angel we hadn't bargained for.

We drove our bounty home and carried the cage to the front door. Carefully opening it, we released Gabriel to join his brothers and brought the kitten inside. Sitting in the lounge chair was the Colombian lady who came once a week to clean our house. Snuggled in her lap was old Abigail, purring like a kitten.

"May I have her? She's so pretty and sweet and my children will love her."

Oh boy. Could she ever! Now we were only stuck with the orphaned ugly one. The creature didn't resemble anything we had ever seen. Its hair ranged from a reddish, burnt auburn to dark brown and stood straight out in thin wisps that gave the appearance of having just been hit by lightning or stuck on a live electrical wire, and its hairless tail was as long as its whole body.

Angel or no angel this one should have been sent to the Humane Society.

Instead we named it "Electric" and took it to my vet who determined it was a 'she' kitten. After he plunged her full of shots, we brought her back home for her first bath. The little feline never complained. *Mom and dad* soaped her up and scrubbed her from top to bottom. She let them do whatever they wanted. She even let herself be brushed. I hated to be brushed and always swung my head to bite the brush and hand that held it. She seemed to love the attention and, when they finished her grooming, she crawled into *dad's* lap and fell asleep.

As dear as she was, she had never lived inside a house and we were nervous about leaving her here with me to take care of. It was decided. She would go to the furniture showroom with *dad*.

Laurel, who managed the front desk, took an immediate liking to the scrawny thing. Her soft Jamaican accent calmed the lively kitten who sat obediently on top of the desk most of the day waiting for Laurel to brush and hand feed her. When

Laurel was busy, Electric jumped on to the deep marble sill of the large picture window that overlooked the street called Decorators' Row. Her wide eyes beckoned the designers and their customers to come on in. She greeted each one as though recognizing a long lost friend, jumping and twirling and comically showing off for their amusement.

In the months that followed, she grew to almost double her original size. Her thin hair thickened to a glossy coat and her tail became an amazing portrait of bi-colored bushy fur that she wrapped around herself when she slept. Even her large ears had tufts of fur inside and on the tips and her round feet had so much tufting they looked as though she was wearing snow shoes. Most notable were her eyes. They had always been large and expressive but now they had a quality of compelling sensitivity that was almost human. She had become a beautiful specimen of something everyone was sure had to be a pedigree.

One afternoon a designer came into the showroom with his client from Maine. She was a lovely lady in her late thirties who carried herself with northeastern elegance. She walked over to electric and scratched the top of her head.

"You are a Maine Coon Cat and a beautiful one at that. How did you find your way to south Florida?"

Everyone in the showroom stopped what they were doing.

"What did you say she is? She's a what??"

"She's a genuine Maine Coon Cat. She's like none other. Her glossy coat is heavy and water resistant to bear the harsh winters, longer on the stomach and britches to protect her from water and snow and shorter on the back so as not to get entangled in the underbrush. Look at her square muzzle. It makes it easier for her to grab moving prey and to lap water from streams. She probably only weighs around ten pounds but looks much larger because of her heavy fur.

She's absolutely marvelous, truly one of the nicest I've seen. She's a rare breed, you know. If you would consider selling her to me, I will take her back to Maine to live with my mother. I fly first class so she will remain with me and not in the baggage compartment of the plane."

It took less than three seconds for everyone to contemplate the offer, during which they thought about the gorgeous Italian silk and French satin damask covered sofas in the showroom that were being torn to smithereens by the Maine beauty's razor sharp claws. Graciously declining any payment for their magnificent specimen, they lovingly kissed Electric good-bye and waived her off first class to her new home.

Maine Lobster for 1ST Classe Coon Cat
Baked Stuffed Maine Lobster
Yield: 1 lobster
Recipe may be multiplied for additional lobsters

1 ½-1 ¾ pound Maine lobster, live

1 tablespoon butter

Lemon to squeeze

1 small shallot, chopped fine

½ celery rib, chopped fine

1 American white mushroom, chopped coarse

4 medium raw shrimp, chopped coarse

2 tablespoons butter

1 tablespoon Pernod

1 tablespoon seasoned bread crumbs

1 tablespoon butter, melted

1. Preheat the oven to 425°F.
2. Prepare the lobster by turning it on its back and plunging a large, sharp knife into the center opening between the eyes. Cut all the way down to the tail. Open the lobster, cracking

the outer shell of the tail so the meat is exposed and the lobster lies flat. This is important so the tail area will not curl during the cooking. Remove the dark, spongy sack just below the eyes where the knife has entered. Remove the vein that runs from the center down the tail. Leave the green tomalley (liver) and any roe intact. Remove the rubber band from the claws and, with the back of the knife, hit the claws hard just to crack.

3. Set the lobster on a baking sheet. Squeeze the lemon over the meat. Brush well with melted butter.
4. Cook the shallot, celery, and mushroom in 2 tablespoons butter over low heat until soft. Stir in the shrimp and Pernod and cook until the shrimp begins to take on color.
5. Stir in the bread crumbs.
6. Spoon in the stuffing, covering the entire lobster, tail and all. Brush with melted butter.
7. Place on the center rack of the oven and bake 15 minutes for 1 ½ pound lobster and 20 minutes for 1 ¾ pounds. If there is no black "mottling" on the claws, it is done. If it does not appear done, reduce the heat to 375°F and bake another 2-3 minutes.

Lobster Bisque Quick and Easy

Yield: 6 cups

Attention: Be very frugal when adding salt
to any shellfish or canned product.

2 – 1½ pound Maine lobsters

Water to fill half a large
soup pot

10-ounce can Campbell's®
Tomato Bisque soup

1½ cups water

14.5 ounce canned finely
diced tomatoes with Italian
herb seasonings

1 tablespoon ground
coriander

¼ teaspoon ground thyme or
several fresh leaves

1 bay leaf

¼ teaspoon hot Hungarian
paprika or a pinch of
cayenne pepper

2 large plum tomatoes,
seeded and diced

3 tablespoons sweet Marsala
or Madeira wine

2 tablespoons or more brandy
or cognac to taste

⅓ cup heavy cream or more
to taste

Salt and a touch of pepper to
taste

Toasted croutons to top

1. Bring water to a boil in a large pot. Plunge lobsters in head
   first. Cover the pot, leaving the cover on a tilt. When the
   water returns to a full boil, lower heat to medium-high so it
   will not boil over the top of the pot. Boil 12 minutes only.
   Remove lobsters to cool to room temperature.
2. Remove meat from the lobsters and cut into small pieces.
   Refrigerate, covered, until ready to serve in the soup.
3. Heat the Tomato Bisque and stir in the water a little at time
   until mixture is smooth. Cut the canned tomatoes into very
   small pieces and add with their juice. Raise heat to medium
   and cook, stirring constantly, until well incorporated.

4. Add cilantro, coriander, ginger, bay leaf, paprika and the diced fresh tomato. Stir in wine and brandy. Reduce heat to very low and cover. Cook 15 minutes.
5. Directly before serving, stir in heavy cream. Bring just to the boiling point, stirring. Stir in the lobster.
6. Serve with croutons to top.
   Note: Steps 1-4 may be done in advance. Always add the cream and lobster directly before serving.

Croutons
Yield: Enough to freeze and use when
needed for soup or salads

1 pound loaf French bread,
    crusts on
2 cloves garlic
1 cup extra virgin olive oil
1 teaspoon dried Italian
    spices

½ teaspoon salt
Optional: ¼ cup freshly
    grated Parmesan or
    Romano cheese

1. With a serrated edge knife, slice the bread in half lengthwise. Leave on the kitchen counter 1 hour to be exposed to the air to harden. Slice each half again two times. Cut into squares, not too small, not too large. Leave on the kitchen counter to be exposed to the air to harden.
2. Peel and slice the garlic. Place in a saucepan with the olive oil. Simmer over very low heat 20-30 minutes. Turn off heat. Allow the mixture to sit 30 minutes longer. Strain into a large bowl or plastic bag. Add the Italian spices and salt.
3. Toss with the bread until all are slightly covered. Remove to a large baking sheet.

4. Preheat oven to 250°F.
5. Leave in the oven 15 minutes. Reduce temperature to 200°F. Leave another 15 minutes, or until crisp and dry. Turn off the oven and leave the croutons inside until they have turned very light brown.
6. Freeze in an airtight container and reheat in a 200°F after defrosting.

"Dogs lives are too short, their only fault, really."
— Agnes Sligh Turnbull

Sam Returns
Home

TOWARD THE END OF SAM'S days the wanderlust from the mixtures of blood that included the Alaskan wolf returned and he obsessively tried to escape his domestic environment. Any time a door was left open he disappeared into the neighborhood. Fortunately, someone always spotted the old white dog and brought him home.

He was almost sixteen and, although he continued to weigh sixty-three pounds and his full coat remained luxuriant, his hips began to fail. Dr. Carson said it was unusual for a dog of his size to live as long as he had. As it became increasingly difficult for him to walk, *dad* carried him to the car each morning to take him to work. He never complained but it was evident he was in distress.

One afternoon, *dad* let Sam out the back door to get some fresh air. When he called for him to come in, he was gone. The gardeners had left the side gate open and he had seized the opportunity to search for his ancestors.

Mom and dad went to all the neighbors and put them on alert. They walked the streets until two o'clock in the morning calling his name. At six o'clock, just as the sun was coming up, the lady from four houses away rang our door bell. Breathlessly, she said that when she and her husband walked out on their dock to watch the sun rise, they saw a white dog treading water in the bay.

"He seems desperately tired. He probably has been in the

water several hours. There's a sandbar there and he must have fallen in during low tide. Now the water is very deep and he's drowning."

Dad quickly changed into his bathing suit and raced along the narrow ledge of the seawall in back of our house. My Sam, too exhausted to stay afloat, was still attempting to tread water. *Dad* dove into the bay and put his body underneath Sam's neck to hold his head above the water. Swimming partially on his back and side while holding Sam with his left arm, he propelled his other arm to maneuver their bodies through the water. The ladder at the end of the dock was too far away to reach and they began to thrash together in the morning high tide at the base of the seawall. Our neighbor ran into her house and returned with a large blanket. She and her husband spread it onto the grass. Holding it by its corners, they created a hammock. Then they lowered it very slightly into the water. *Dad* somehow tucked Sam into it. They pulled simultaneously, slowly bringing Sam upward. The blanket wobbled and, for a minute, looked as though it could not hold his weight and he would fall back into the bay. Because he was in shock, he didn't attempt to move and they continued pulling him to the top of the seawall and finally, with great effort, onto the grass. Another blanket was brought and they wrapped it around his shaking, wet body. *Dad* swam to the dock where he climbed the ladder and joined them.

Another neighbor brought his van and made a bed for Sam in the back. *Mom* and *dad* crawled in and cushioned his head and shoulders on their laps.

Dr. Carson was waiting for them with two nurses outside his hospital. Sam was hurriedly carried to an examining room where his vital signs were checked. One nurse took his temperature while the other hooked up an IV with glucose and water and inserted it into the jugular vein in his neck. He remained on his side deathly still, his eyes sort of dreamy and glazed, but he was breathing.

"Would you like to leave him here or take him home", asked the doctor?

"Take him home."

"I will give you enough glucose refills to feed him for forty-eight hours. The solution will bring him out of his shock."

He showed them how to unhook the bag when it was empty and connect a full one into the tube connected to his vein.

"Call me if there's a turn for the worse. He's a good strong animal. I think he will come out of this."

The three of us stayed beside him throughout the day and all that night. The next morning he drank water on his own and stood up for a few minutes as we cheered his recovery.

He lived another six months but he never really recovered. He was too tired to go to the showroom again and remained at home for *mom* and me to take care of while *dad* went to work alone. As the weeks lengthened into months, he could no longer stand. When *dad* was home, he carried him outside, but he was too heavy and awkward for mom to lift, so she kept him in the kitchen with a heavy towel under him to keep him dry and clean. I licked his stomach and legs clean several times a day and he moved his tail with gratitude. Twice each week he was taken to Dr. Carson for a shot of cortisone to ease the pain of arthritis and another to keep him from becoming dehydrated. His eyes begged to be released from this world and we all knew it would be an act of kindness to end his suffering. *Dad* wrestled with losing his best friend until he finally came to terms with the knowledge that real love was not holding on for oneself but letting go for another.

Mom drove Sam to the doctor for the last time. She kissed his forehead and laid her cheek against his face while the doctor prepared the syringe. Sam licked her hand as though to say, *thank you*. Then he closed his eyes and waited for peace to come to his old body.

Cats don't usually show their inner feelings but the family saw that I was in mourning. I had not only lost my best friend, I had lost my soul-mate. Would I have to wait another three hundred years for us to be together as the white dog and white cat of Indian legend? I slept the next week without interest in food or play. And then one morning it was over and I returned to the family.

"There can be no joy without food and drink"
— Talmud, Mo'ed Katan

Sakie Visits So-Be 1993 and finds South Beach 1970

MIAMI BEACH MUST BE THE most unique city in the whole world. Tourists from the States, Canada, South America, Europe and Asia bask in the sun, shop the shops, and spend $20 to park at restaurants that feature fancy lettuce like Batavia on their menus. Long-legged model types in skin tight designer jeans stroll through the outdoor mall of the Bal Harbour Shops carrying long garment bags that announce there is going to be an upcoming event. There is always an upcoming event somewhere on Miami Beach that requires serious preparation.

Everyone seems to have loads of money on this island where pretension reigns supreme and lots of folks bring their dogs to accompany them on these shopping expeditions. They're not actually real dogs, just as the people aren't real people. Tiny and fluffy, they have bows connected to puffs of fur that stick straight up from the tops of their heads and blue toenails that peek out from coiffed paws. They are perfectly sized to fit into Chanel, Hermes, Vuitton, and Gucci shoulder bags.

Because I am now five years old and very well-mannered, *mom* decides to take me with her to review the most popular restaurant in the mall for her newspaper. The indoor-outdoor Italian eatery that faces the parking lot can be seen all the way from Collins Avenue. The circular outdoor area is the nucleus where people watch people while they nurse huge glasses of wine at affordable prices.

She walks me on a leash from her car to the table trying to

hide her amusement as people gawk at the twenty-two pound cat with white fur that brushes the ground. Then she picks me up, removes the leash and places me on the chair next to her where I sit perfectly erect in my signature Bobtail stance. The owner knows that she and her friend, Carole, are the Zagat Restaurant Survey editors and comes out to greet us. Then he announces in a voice audible to the other tables, "Let's see if our fish of the day is acceptable to Sakie". And, of course it is. Grilled or blackened, sautéed or fried – alone or topped with giant prawns, *Carpaccio Ristorante* could incite any cat to riot from the fragrance of this fish that seems to have jumped from the ocean directly into the pan. The fancy side salad of chopped arugula tossed with small squares of watermelon, yellow pepper, black seedless grapes and feta cheese in a light Asian dressing with a touch of sweet ginger is appreciatively devoured by *mom*.

We finish our lunch and return to the car to drive the seven mile length of Miami Beach to the Art Deco area, once called South Beach, now known as SoBe. We cruise Indian Creek Drive past the *Surfside 6* Houseboat from the television show was docked in the early 1960s. We pass the huge Fontainebleau Hotel bus drivers once announced as "Yankee Stadium". *Mom* points to a street called Arthur Godfrey Road that was named during the 1950s to honor the man who broadcast a popular radio show from the Kenilworth Hotel. As the creek narrows, the hotels and apartment buildings become smaller and shabby. We see that some have been bought by developers and are brightly colored. The Hotel, The National and The Claridge have been placed on the list of Historic Hotels of the United States and refurbished to reflect their elegant past. Others have been and will continue to be torn down and replaced with multi-million dollar structures that will draw a young international crowd.

She tells me about her first visit to the old South Beach in 1970 when she was sent by The Sun Reporter Newspaper to interview elderly ladies for Passover recipes. Then she begins to talk about a lady named Barbara Capitman, who died in March at the age of 69 when she still had so much to accomplish. She recalls the day she met her in 1976 when the interior designers came together for their very first meeting in the' restaurant at *dad's* furniture showroom, *Imports for the Trade*, to put into formation the Miami Design Preservation League. Every decorator and store owner in the design district from the elegant showrooms that lined 40th Street to the warehouses on 25th street and North Miami Avenue gathered to listen to her determination to save the buildings built in the 1930s to look like ocean liners and rocket ships. Because she spoke in a raspy faltering staccato, she gave the impression of being rather strange or delusional and the Miami Beach City Manager and developers awaiting demolition crews refused to listen to the "crazy" preservationist, who was later immortalized as an *intrepid little old lady* by the <u>Los Angeles Times</u>."

"We set out platters of cheese and bread on each table and filled the buffet with fruit, soft drinks and wine. The meeting that began at four o'clock on a Friday afternoon was still in full swing at eight o'clock. No one wanted to leave and it was after the dinner hour so we served the turkey and coleslaw designated for the next day's lunch. The camaraderie and cohesiveness of this group that pledged to stand behind and fight for Barbara Capitman's dream was sealed forever.

It was because of her that the area is the only district with 20th Century architecture in the Historic Register," said *mom*, with pride of having been a small part of such an important movement.

Mom takes one hand off the wheel and points to a rundown

building on the corner of Washington Avenue and 18th Street. "See that building, Sakie. There used to be a huge colored neon sign flashing, Pickin' Chicken, the restaurant owned by the man who later built the Castaways Hotel. During the 1950s, the area was the restaurant nucleus of the city. Local residents stood in line at Embers Steak House, the Park Avenue, Il Piccolo's Italian, and the immortal Wolfie's for sandwiches too thick to fit into your mouth. *Dad* grew up on the Beach and could write an entire book of stories about how things were in the 1940s and '50s. He was a mascot for the army troops stationed on Miami Beach during World War II. They carried him on their shoulders when they marched down Collins Avenue."

"Look to the right, Sakie. That's the Lincoln Road Mall. I remember when they closed the street to traffic almost twenty years ago. Everyone said the businesses would go bankrupt when people could not drive by to see what was there. For a little while, they were right. Bonwit Teller moved out immediately. Saks 5th Avenue remained for almost fifteen more years because it had a parking lot behind it, but Moseley's Fine Linens still remains as it has for three generations as a landmark for hand embroidered tablecloths and monogrammed sheets and towels for elegant homes and bride trousseaus. The mall will never become a Bal Harbour but it will be a popular area for restaurants and antique shops in the future.

I am sorry to say that I have lost interest and fallen asleep while she is reminiscing. Then, suddenly, she stops the car. "We're here, Sakie." I look up. The sign says, Ocean Drive. There are buildings painted in garish colors with flashy signs all heaped together on one side of the street and a long stretch of sand that leads to the ocean on the other. The people are all heaped together also, lying in the sand or eating and drinking shoulder to shoulder at tables covered by umbrellas.

She fastens my leash and sets me on the sidewalk. There is something about this place that makes me nervous and I sit down. All of a sudden I hear what sounds like thunder coming from the ground behind me. Three disreputable looking figures in bathing trunks and long hair with feet attached to wood planks on wheels are closing in on us. I howl but no one hears me as the roller blades circle around us. I freak out and break the collar from around my neck to dive under the nearest table. *Mom* tries to grab me and I run between the buildings to hide.

Shaking uncontrollably, I cower with my eyes closed. I hear a small meow and look up to see a very old cat.

It's OK, she says. *There's nothing to be afraid of. This is the new South Beach. They call it SoBe. It's also called the Art Deco Area. It's a bit strange and some of the side streets are dark and foreboding, but Ocean Drive is what they call a "Happening".*

What do you mean, a 'happening'? What is happening, I ask.

A Happening is a spontaneous event where everyone participates. Look at these people participating for no reason other than they all came to see and be seen in a new and bizarre atmosphere where everyone is young. Do you see that beautiful couple sitting at a table for two under the umbrella?

I do. They are indeed handsome humans, she with long hair like my Susan and he, obviously a person of means judging from the $200 bottle of 1990 Stag's Leap Cellars Estate Cask 23

Cabernet Sauvignon from Napa Valley that breathes on the table between them. Something, however, is amiss with the picture.

But they're not talking to each other, I say, *they're typing something into Nokia cell phones with their thumbs.*

Indeed, she answers, *they are learning to text SMS messages through Nokia's Communicator, the new GSM invention. If the technology continues, face to face communication could become a major problem. I suppose this new interaction will be no less enjoyable than what existed between young lovers of past generations. It will just be different. It's part of the happening.*

Since I did not understand, I thought it best to return to my own thoughts. *But, what became of all the old people? My human mom collected Passover recipes here in 1970 from elderly Jewish ladies who lived here.*

Let me tell you a story.
Fifteen years ago, in 1978, someone dumped me on this street. Because I was a cute kitten, I found lots of people to give me food. But the best dinners were made by a Jewish lady who had also been dumped here by her children. We immediately bonded. At first, she fed me leftovers on the porch of the dilapidated two story apartment building where she lived. When I let her know I appreciated her friendship, she brought me inside. For the next eight years we ate dinner together in her tiny kitchen. Oh, what a cook she was! She could have opened a kosher gourmet destination

better than the Famous Restaurant on Washington Avenue. I will always remember her crunchy potato pancakes and tender brisket of beef that she sliced thin and covered with brown gravy. She always served it with a carrot-sweet potato casserole she called "Tzsimmis". During the week of Passover when we were not allowed to have any flour, she made me pancakes from a large cracker she broke up and dipped into beaten eggs that she called matzo brei. And, she made balls out of fresh fish she called gefüllte when all her friends were buying them bottled. The entire apartment building was permeated with the marvelous odor of boiled fish bones for days. Everyone complained because they were jealous, but we didn't care. We just snuggled up together and enjoyed.

Hanukah was my favorite holiday. She had a candle-thing she called a Menorah that had eight holders and a ninth to light them from. Years ago, during my second life back in 165 BCE, my people won a battle to take back their temple in Jerusalem from the Greeks who were worshiping idols. Only one flask of oil could be found to rekindle the eternal light. The oil lasted eight days during which time a new supply was purified. We dedicated the miracle as The Festival of Lights that we have celebrated for over two thousand years.

What do you mean, "My people"? You're not Jewish. You're a cat. Cats can't be Jewish.

You're wrong, little Pagan cat. Once you have a Jewish mom, you will always be Jewish.

Don't call me a Pagan, I hiss. *If you're a Jewish cat, then I'm a Christian cat.*

Wrong again. I have always had a Jewish human mom. I remember you from my first life. You were the mau of Ramses daughter when I was the favorite cat of Moses' wife. The Egyptians were Pagans so you're a Pagan. You are what your first mom was and that makes you a Pagan.

I wasn't going to argue with a cat that had an attitude of superiority, particularly one who was my elder. Besides, she was really interesting and I did not want her to walk away and leave me without my present *mom* in that crazy neighborhood.

Please, I beg in a soft voice, *tell me what the lady cooked for you during the week of Hanukah.*

She lets out a purr that sounds like a happy gurgle and continues:

We dined on fluffy matzo balls bobbing in rich homemade chicken soup and crêpes with chicken broth instead of milk so they would be kosher to fill with gingered chicken.

So, what happened to your elderly lady? Did she die?

No, she was quite healthy but, when the city told her children the building was to be renovated and she would have to move out, they came and took her away to a nursing home.

But, that's awful, I exclaim. *She must have known they wouldn't allow her to do her own cooking there. She must have been terribly unhappy.*

True you are, little Pagan. She cried for weeks holding me in her lap saying she didn't care about herself but was worried who would feed her Jewish cat. I let her know that I would miss her but would be safe in the neighborhood.

And, have you been safe here? It's so noisy and crowded for a cat alone. Everyone seems to be preoccupied or participating in the "happening", as you have said.

She looks at me with that expression of superiority again before answering.

I have been in this neighborhood fifteen years. The restaurant owners all know me and let me sample their recipes of New American Cuisine before serving it to their customers. They make me special servings of blackened grouper and salmon fillets baked over fennel and yellow peppers with fried polenta on the side. Sometimes the chef will set it over a salad of black beans and mango with a spoonful of lump crab on top of the polenta cake. I've also learned to eat grilled pork chops with mango sauce and sautéed giant shrimp with tabouli. It may not be kosher but I've come to believe this new cuisine is almost as good as that prepared by my lady.

My Best Life

*But, what was wrong with the other food? Why
don't they eat matzo balls and tzsimmis and boiled
fish balls any longer?*

*Now, that's a very good question. Since you seem
to be an amateur historian, you must have noticed
that food has always been an integral part of events
through the ages. Food is history itself. For example,
Columbus landed in America by mistake when he
traveled west to find a new route to the East Indies
for spices after the Ottoman Empire blocked the spice
trade route. Did you know that rice and coffee and
melons and dates were carried back to Europe from
the Middle East during the Crusades? And, the
world would never have had French fries had it
not been for Antoine August Parmentier, a French
chemist captured by the Germans in the Seven
Years' War in the late 1750s. While in prison, he
was fed only potatoes, a food for cattle. When he
was released, he brought some back to France and
presented Queen Marie Antoinette with a bouquet
of potato flowers. She put them in her hair and
they immediately became a fashion statement for her
court. King Louis gave him land to plant the tubers
that later saved the entire country from starvation.
By the middle of 1800, deep fried potatoes had
become a fad food in France and Belgium. It is said
that American soldiers stationed in France during
World War I brought the recipe back to the States.
And the bagel that has become the college food staple
was brought to America by Jewish immigrants
from Poland in the 1880's. And, it's because slaves*

186

*were brought from Africa that Americans became
aware of their diet of legumes, grains, vegetables
and greens that made them healthier than the diet of
fatty foods that shortened their masters' lives. And,
now that everyone is health conscious, greasy foods
and heavy meats and gravies are disappearing from
restaurant menus.*

*So, has all the food that people once enjoyed gone out
of style,* I ask?

*Not all the food; only some. Chocolate will never
go out of style. Look at the crowd at those tables.
They're devouring chocolate soufflés and undercooked
hot chocolate brownies. Now look at the people on
the beach. They're licking chocolate ice cream cones.
Chocolate was invented 3100 years ago by the Aztecs
and introduced into Europe in the 16th century by
the Spanish. The one food people through the ages
have never given up is chocolate and I think it will
be that way forever.*

This has been most enlightening, I purr, *but I think
I should go home to my quiet neighborhood. Thank
you for telling me your story.*

I spot *mom* frantically searching for me under the tables
and walk casually from the space between the buildings to sit
behind her. When she turns around, she grabs me into her
arms and runs to the car. She didn't have a chance to interview
anyone because of me. I had ruined her day. I wish I could
speak human language because I have a better column for her

newspaper than she could ever have gotten from any of the new SoBe crowd that took over South Beach.

South Beach Matzo Balls
Yield: 18-20
These may be served in soup or as a side
dumpling with chicken, meat or fish

4 jumbo eggs
1 cup sifted matzo meal
¾ teaspoon salt
⅛ teaspoon white pepper
¼ teaspoon grated nutmeg
Optional: 1 tablespoon finely-chopped parsley or chervil
8 tablespoons rendered chicken fat or refrigerated

fat that has risen to the top of the soup.
2 tablespoons seltzer water or club soda
A solution of 1 quart water mixed with 1 quart canned chicken broth to cook them, or 2 quarts vegetable broth.

1. To render the fat: Place the fat removed from the chicken into a saucepan. Add salt, pepper, a little chopped onion and celery. Cook over very low heat until the fat is extracted. Allow it to rest several hours before straining. Discard the fat pieces.
2. Beat the eggs. Stir in matzo meal, salt, pepper and nutmeg (parsley). Stir in melted fat or butter until completely mixed. Stir in seltzer water. Refrigerate several hours or overnight.
3. Bring the water and broth to a boil. Dip your hands in ice water and form balls the size of large walnuts. Drop into the boiling liquid. Boil hard, uncovered, 5 minutes. Place a cover on a tilt to allow air space for steam to escape. Boil hard 10 minutes. Reduce heat to medium high, making

sure liquid is at a full boil. Boil at least 45 minutes. Cut one in half. When color is opaque throughout with no wet look in the center, they are done.

4. Carefully remove the balls with a slotted spoon to the hot chicken soup where they will absorb the flavor. Or, leave them in the liquid until ready to serve as a side dumpling.
5. Note: Three secrets of light matzo balls are: The addition of seltzer water, cold balls dropped into the boiling liquid, and the water remaining at a rolling boil throughout the cooking process.

Traditional Chicken Soup
Reduced fat
Yield: Approximately 14 cups

6-8 pound stew chicken, or 2 chickens weighing 4 pounds each
6 leeks, white part only
2 large white onions, peeled and cut into quarters
Optional: 2 cloves garlic, peeled and split

Bottom of whole celery plus 2 ribs, cut up
2 whole cloves
1 bunch parsley
1 bunch dill weed
2 teaspoons kosher salt
1 teaspoon black pepper
5 quarts cool water
4-5 whole carrots

1. Remove the skin and as much fat as possible from the chicken. If necessary, cut the chicken in half or quarters to fit into your soup pot.
2. Preheat oven to 375°F.
3. Place the white part of the leeks on aluminum foil and roast until they turn color, approximately twenty minutes. (The

roasted leek is one of the secrets of the French soup, Petite Marmite.)

4. Combine the leek with remaining ingredients in a large pot, reserving the carrots for later. Skim off any dark froth that bubbles on top. Cover. Reduce heat to medium-high. Boil gently for 2 hours.

5. Cool to room temperature. Strain and refrigerate several hours or overnight. Remove some of the white meat and cube or slice to add to the soup. Do not add until directly before serving.

6. Peel, slice and cook the carrots and any other vegetables you plan to add.

7. Bring the completed soup with its vegetables and reserved chicken to a boil. Taste. Correct the seasoning and ladle into individual soup bowls or serve from a soup tureen at the table.

Note: Be careful when adding salt. It is better to add less than too much. Palates that require more can add it at the table.

Matzo Brei
Yield: Approximately 2 servings

2 jumbo eggs	2 tablespoons butter
Optional: 1 drop vanilla extract	1 tablespoon sifted powdered sugar
2 pieces whole matzos	⅛ teaspoon cinnamon
Sprinkling of salt and pepper	

1. Break matzos into small pieces and place in a strainer or colander. Pour boiling water over to soften. Allow to stand 10 minutes. Squeeze out water.

2. In a fairly large bowl, beat eggs (Add vanilla). Sprinkle with salt and pepper. Stir in softened matzo pieces. Allow to stand 15 minutes.
3. Heat the butter in a skillet or on a griddle. Pour in the matzo/egg mixture. Cook over low heat until omelet is set. Fold in half or turn over. Do not overcook.
4. Mix the sugar and cinnamon together and sprinkle over the omelet. Divide omelet into 2 portions.
5. Serve with jam, syrup, applesauce or honey on the side.
6. Note: Mixture may also be scrambled, omitting or incorporating the sugar/cinnamon during the cooking process.

Gefüllte Fish
Yield: 12 good-sized balls
The amount of fish is determined by its weight
before the head, bones and skin are removed.

3 pounds firm whitefish or cod or flounder with head and bones, skin discarded
1 pound trout or pike with head and bones, cleaned well
2 large shallots
1 large sweet onion, such as Vidalia or Texas white
2 teaspoons salt

½ teaspoon white pepper
1 tablespoon white sugar
⅓ cup cold seltzer water or club soda
¼ cup matzo meal, unsifted, or ¼ cup fine breadcrumbs
3 egg whites

3-4 large carrots

1. Have the fish department at the store remove the head and bones and discard the skin if scales have not been removed.

2. Put the raw fish flesh, shallots, onion, salt, pepper and sugar though a grinder or into a food processor with the steel blade to pulverize. Add the seltzer and matzo meal, turning the processor on-off until combined. Or, mix these in by hand.
3. Beat the egg whites until thick and fold into the fish mixture. Refrigerate while making the fish stock.
4. Boil the carrots whole in water to cover until tender. Drain and refrigerate.

Fish Stock

Head and bones from the fish (and skin, if scales have been removed)
3-4 celery ribs with leaves
Bunch of parsley
Handful of fresh dill

1 whole garlic clove, peeled
1 bay leaf
1 tablespoon salt
1 teaspoon white pepper
1 gallon cold water

1. Boil the ingredients for the fish stock in a large soup pot for 1½ hours. Cool to room temperature. Strain two times to make sure there are no bones. Return strained stock to the pot.
2. Bring the fish stock to a boil. Form fish into 12-14 oblongs 3" X 2" and drop them one at a time carefully into the stock. Cover the pot, leaving it tilted to let a little steam escape. Reduce the heat just enough so the balls boil gently. Cook 1½ hours. Remove one of the balls and cut it in half to check for doneness. If it is not done enough, return it to the stock and boil one-half hour longer. If it is done, turn off heat, cover the pot and allow the balls to cool to room temperature. When they are cool, remove them to glass

containers. Pour the stock over and refrigerate 24 hours or longer for the flavors to blend.

To Serve: Cut the carrots into halves lengthwise or slice into 1 inch pieces with a serrated knife. Place fish on a platter garnished with baby greens, romaine lettuce and fresh dill. Set the carrots around and pass accompanied by a sauceboat of red horseradish.

Note: The fish stock should reduce considerably while it cooks and become clear gelatin in the refrigerator. Cut it into squares to put on the platter with the fish and carrots. It is truly a delicacy.

Shortcut Fish Balls

1 ½ pounds whitefish, cod or scrod fillets

½ pound trout, pike, or flounder fillets

1 large or 2 small shallots

1 medium sweet onion, such as Vidalia, Texas white or Florida Sorrento

1 teaspoon salt

¼ teaspoon white pepper

2 teaspoons granulated sugar

3 tablespoons cold seltzer water or club soda

⅛ cup un-sifted matzo meal

1 jumbo egg white

1 quart vegetable broth

1 quart water

Optional: 2 envelopes unflavored gelatin (Homemade fish stock becomes gelatin)

1. Put raw fish fillets into a food processor or grinder with the shallots, onion, salt, pepper and sugar. Add seltzer and matzo meal.
2. Beat egg white until thick ant stir into fish mixture. Refrigerate until cold.

3. Bring vegetable broth and water to a full boil. Shape cold fish into balls (wetting your hands) and drop, one at a time, into the boiling liquid. Cover the pot, leaving the top tilted to allow a little steam to escape. Reduce heat just enough so galls boil gently. Cook 1 ½ hours.
4. Remove pot from heat and allow fish to cool in the liquid. Remove fish balls to a container with a slotted spoon.
5. Strain 2 cups of the liquid into another pot. Stir in 2 envelopes unflavored kosher gelatin and bring to a boil, stirring. Cool and pour over fish. Refrigerate overnight. Serve with horseradish and boiled carrots.
Note: Gelatin is not kosher unless marked. Kosher gelatin is not vegetarian.

Brisket (Breast of Beef)
Yield: 6-8 servings

3-4 pounds 1st cut brisket of beef
Salt and pepper
3 large carrots, minced
1 large onion, minced
2 cloves garlic, crushed
1 cup concentrated beef broth
1¼ cup water
¼ cup dry red wine
3 fresh bay leaves or 1 dried

2 tablespoons dark brown sugar
½ teaspoon ground cloves
½ teaspoon ground allspice
2 tablespoons tomato ketchup
2 tablespoons all-purpose flour or 1 tablespoon sifted potato starch
1 cup cold water

1. Preheat oven to 350°F.
2. Cross cut slits into the fat of the meat. Season all over with salt and pepper. Set into a roasting pan fat side up.

3. Mince the carrots and onion in a food processor. Remove to a bowl. Stir in the garlic, beef broth, water, (red wine) and bay leaf. Pour over the brisket.
4. Combine the brown sugar with the cloves, allspice and ketchup and rub well into the top of the beef.
5. Cover the roasting pan and cook 3 hours, or until very tender. Remove the beef to a platter or deep dish. Strain the gravy into a container. Cover both and refrigerate until the fat has congealed at the top of the gravy.
6. Combine the flour (potato starch) with the water, stirring until smooth. Pour the gravy into a saucepan. Stir in the flour mixture and bring to a boil, stirring.
7. Slice the cold brisket across the grain and place into a baking dish. Pour the gravy over and reheat in the oven, covered.
8. Serve with browned potatoes or potato pancakes and applesauce.

Potato Pancakes
(Yiddish Latkes, German Kartoffelpuffer)
Yield: Approximately 6-10 pancakes

The potatoes must be cooked immediately after grating so they do not turn black when exposure to air oxidizes them.

2 tablespoons sifted all-purpose flour or 1 full tablespoon potato flour or matzo meal
1 teaspoon baking powder (Exchange for ¼ teaspoon baking soda + ½ teaspoon cream of tartar during Passover)
1 teaspoon salt or more to taste
Pinch of white pepper
1 small onion, chopped fine
1 jumbo egg, beaten

1 pound Russet or Idaho potatoes (best choice because the starch holds the pancake together)

Vegetable oil just to cover the bottom of a large non-stick skillet

1. Combine the flour, baking powder, salt and white pepper in a bowl.
2. Peel the onion and chop fine or pulverize in a food processor. Add the egg and turn the machine on-off. Add the flour mixture. Turn the machine on-off.
3. Peel the potatoes and shred them over the large side of the shredder into a bowl.
4. Stir in the onion mixture.
5. Cover the bottom of a non-stick skillet with vegetable or olive oil over medium-high heat. When it begins to sizzle, drop the batter by large tablespoons or a small ice cream scoop into the sizzling vegetable oil. Flatten with the back of a spoon. Cook, uncovered, until brown on both sides. Drain on paper toweling.
6. If you have an oven with a warmer, set the pancakes into it uncovered. If not, keep in a warm place until ready to serve.
7. Serve with warm applesauce.

Sweet Potato-Carrot Tzimmes
Yield: 6 servings

3 medium-size sweet potatoes
16 ounce package baby
  Belgian carrots
6 ounce package dried
  apricots
¼ cup honey
½ teaspoon cinnamon

⅛ teaspoon nutmeg
1 tablespoon light brown
  sugar
¼ teaspoon salt
3 tablespoons orange juice
Light brown sugar to sprinkle
  over the top

1. Boil sweet potatoes until done but still firm. Peel and slice into halves lengthwise.
   Boil carrots until tender.
2. Soak apricots in warm water 10 minutes, or until soft. Slice into halves.
3. Combine honey, cinnamon, nutmeg, sugar, salt and orange juice, stirring until blended. Spoon into a shallow round casserole.
4. Set sweet potatoes around, with narrow ends pointing inward. Combine carrots and apricots and set in-between potato slices. Spoon sauce over all.
5. Preheat oven to 350 F. Sprinkle with sugar and bake 10 minutes, or until very hot.

Chicken Broth Crêpes
Yield: Approximately 24 crêpes

3 jumbo eggs
2 jumbo egg yolks
½ teaspoon salt
¼ teaspoon black pepper
1 tablespoon dry sherry

1 ½ cups all-purpose flour or
    ¾ cup + 1 tablespoon potato
    flour, sifted 3 times
2 ½ cup rich chicken broth
¼ cup butter substitute,
    melted

1. Beat the eggs and yolks with the salt, pepper and sherry until blended.
2. Add the flour and the chicken broth in thirds, beating after each addition until thick and smooth. Add the butter. Pour the batter into a cup with a spout.
3. Heat a non-stick frying pan or crêpe pan no larger than 6-7 inches in diameter. Pour in enough batter to cover the bottom and immediately pour any excess batter back into the cup. Allow the batter to set and then cut around the edge to remove the batter stuck to the side. Cook only until set. The bottom will just be taking on color. Chicken broth crêpes take longer to cook than those made with milk. Do not remove the crêpe too soon or it will break apart. Turn the crêpe over and cook just until the surface is dry. Set on wax paper to cool. Stack.
4. Fill with Chicken Ginger recipe below.

Ginger Chicken

Yield: Approximately 6 cups chicken to fill 24 crêpes

4 whole chicken breasts, skinned and boned
Salt, pepper to sprinkle
¼ cup olive oil
2 shallots, finely diced
2 tablespoons finely-diced ginger
2 ½ cups chicken broth
½ cup chardonnay wine

½ pound sliced American white or fresh morel mushrooms
2 tablespoons butter or butter substitute
3 tablespoons all-purpose flour
⅛ teaspoon cayenne pepper or hot Hungarian paprika

1. Salt and pepper the chicken breasts.
2. Heat the olive oil and simmer the shallots until they become soft but not colored.
3. Add the chicken breasts and ginger. Add 1 ½ cups of the chicken broth and all the wine. Cover and cook over medium heat about 20 minutes, or until the chicken is cooked. Remove the chicken to cool and strain the sauce. Slice the chicken into strips and set aside.
4. Sauté the mushrooms in the butter or butter substitute. Stir in the flour. Add the remaining broth and stir until smooth. Pour it into the strained sauce and bring to a boil, stirring until thick and smooth.
5. Place a good amount of chicken in the center of the un-cooked side of each crêpe. Spoon some of the sauce over and close one side of the crêpe over. Close the other side over the first. Place flap side down on an oiled, sided cookie sheet. Brush each crêpe with a little melted butter or butter substitute.

6. Bake in a preheated 350°F oven until hot.
7. Place 2 crêpes on each plate or a heated platter and spoon some sauce over.

So-Be It Grouper
Yield: 4 servings

4 grouper fillets, 6 ounces each
1 lime

1teaspoon butter
2 teaspoons olive oil
1 lemon, quartered

Blackened Seasoning
Combine:
1 teaspoon paprika
½ teaspoon garlic salt
½ teaspoon onion powder

¼ teaspoon chili powder
1 teaspoon black pepper
¼ teaspoon cayenne pepper

1. Rub the top of the fillets with the seasoning. Squeeze lime juice over.
2. Heat butter and olive oil on a griddle or non-stick skillet over medium.
3. Sear the grouper on the underside without the rub until brown. Turn and sear the top side until a fork flakes the fish without opaque color. Do not overcook.
Serve with Sautéed Bananas.

Banana Sauce
Yield: 4 servings

4 South Florida "Finger" or Dwarf Cavendish bananas, yellow but firm

4 tablespoons unsalted butter

3 tablespoons light brown sugar

2 teaspoons grated orange rind

A pinch of freshly grated nutmeg

¼ teaspoon cinnamon

⅓ cup orange juice

1 tablespoon lemon juice

⅓ cup banana liqueur

1. Melt butter with the sugar, orange rind, nutmeg and sugar in a shallow pan. Add the orange and lemon juice and cook, stirring, until hot.
2. Slice the bananas lengthwise and place them into the pan, spooning the mixture over. Turn the bananas over one time and cook approximately 5 minutes, or until they begin to soften.. Pour the banana liqueur over the bananas into the sauce. Spoon over the bananas.
3. Divide the sauce onto 4 plates. Set a fish fillet of blackened grouper in the center with a banana half on each side.

Salmon Baked with Fennel and Peppers
Yield: 4 servings

4 salmon fillets, 6 ounces each, skin removed

Salt and pepper

1 fennel bulb, sliced into long thin strips

1 yellow bell pepper, sliced into long thin strips

1 orange bell pepper, sliced into long thin strips

½ cup chopped scallion greens

Juice of 1 lemon

¼ pound butter, melted

½ cup dry white wine

1 cup seasoned panko bread crumbs

1. Preheat oven to 425°F.
2. Slice the fennel on the round into long thin strips. Slice the peppers into long thin strips. Chop the scallion greens.
3. Wash and dry the salmon fillets. Sprinkle lightly on both sides with salt and pepper.
4. Brush the fillets heavily on both sides with lemon juice and melted butter.
5. Pour remaining butter into a shallow casserole dish. Stir in the wine.
6. Arrange the fennel, peppers, and scallions into 4 piles and set the fillets on top, skin-side down.
7. Press the panko crumbs heavily over the fillets.
8. Bake 10-12 minutes until no sign of red remains when flaked with a fork. Do not overcook. Remove to individual plates with a spatula and spoon the sauce over the tops.
9. Decorate the tops with some of the green fennel fronds.

Fried Polenta
Yield: 8 large or 12 small cakes

1 cup yellow cornmeal   ⅛ teaspoon white pepper
3 cups cool water   ¼ teaspoon ground cumin
⅓ teaspoon garlic salt   ¼ teaspoon ground coriander
Optional: Chopped arugula tossed with black beans, chopped
fresh mango and bottled Asian dressing mixed with a small
amount of mango jam and Chinese sweet and sour sauce to taste.
Optional: Lump crab to top

1. Combine the cornmeal with the garlic salt, white pepper,
   cumin, and coriander. Stir into the water and bring to a
   slow boil.
2. Reduce heat to very low immediately and continue to cook,
   stirring in one direction only, until mixture is very thick and
   smooth. Remove from the stove and spoon into a square
   9X9 inch baking pan, smoothing it evenly. Set aside to cool
   completely. Refrigerate until very cold.

Peanut or canola oil to just coat the bottom of a non-stick skillet
1 jumbo egg white beaten to the frothy stage
Unseasoned bread crumbs to dredge

1. Cut the polenta into 8 equal pieces.
2. Pour the oil into a non-stick shallow skillet over medium
   heat.
3. Dip the polenta pieces into the egg white and then into the
   crumbs.

4. Fry them until brown and crisp. Drain on paper toweling. Set 1 or 2 of the cakes on the chopped arugula mixture. Top with a spoonful of crab meat.
5. Optional: Toss a few mixed greens with black beans and chopped fresh mango in a very sparse amount of the dressing. Set a polenta cake on top. Spoon a dollop of crab on top of the polenta.

FOR THE BLACK BEANS: Wash 1 cup dried black beans and pour into a pot. Pour 3 cups boiling water over. Add 1 whole clove peeled garlic and 1 teaspoon salt. Bring to a boil. Reduce heat to low. Cook covered, until beans become soft for approximately 1 hour. Remove the garlic clove. Drain off any excess water. Refrigerate beans until ready to use.

Sautéed Shrimp with Tabbouleh
Yield: 4 servings

16 very large shrimp, 15 to the pound

4 tablespoons butter, melted
2 tablespoons dry white wine

1. Remove shells and devein shrimp, leaving tails intact. Marinate in the melted butter 15 minutes, turning frequently.
2. Heat a grill pan and quickly sear the shrimp on both sides. Add the butter in which they marinated and the wine and bring to a boil. When they turn pink, remove the shrimp with tongs to serve immediately over the tabbouleh.
Note: This may also be served cold with the shrimp tossed with the tabbouleh. Toast French bread slices and brush with the butter-wine mixture from the shrimp.

Tabbouleh
Yield: 4 servings

½ cup cooked bulgur or barley

1 tablespoon lemon juice

1 cup chopped plum tomatoes

1 cup chopped purple onion

1½ cups chopped curly parsley

¼ cup minced fresh mint leaves

¼ cup minced fresh basil leaves

2 tablespoons extra-virgin olive oil

1 small clove garlic, minced

1 teaspoon kosher salt

½ teaspoon minced Anaheim green mild chili pepper

Optional: Pinch of cayenne or hot Hungarian paprika

Optional: Peeled and seeded chopped cucumber

1. Pour boiling water over the bulgur to soften or cook the barley in water to cover until done but still firm. Set aside.
2. Combine the lemon juice, tomatoes, onion, parsley, mint and basil in a bowl. Allow it to sit 10 minutes. Drain off the water that will gather from the tomatoes. Stir in the olive oil, garlic, salt, pepper, cayenne and paprika. Stir in the bulgur (barley). Refrigerate several hours or overnight. Note: Do not incorporate cucumber until directly before serving or mixture will become watery.

Grilled Pork Chops with Mango Sauce
Yield: 4 servings

4 center cut rib pork chops,
6-8 ounces each
Salt, pepper

1 teaspoon extra virgin
olive oil
¼ cup dry white wine
½ cup rich chicken broth

1. Sprinkle the chops with salt and pepper.
2. Rub a non-stick skillet or grill pan with oil.
3. Heat the pan over high.
4. Grill the chops on both sides until seared.
5. Add the wine. Bring to a boil. Add the broth. Reduce heat to simmer.
6. Cover the pan and simmer on lowest temperature until tender.
7. Remove to individual plates and spoon Mango Sauce over.

Mango Sauce
Yield: 2 cups

2 large ripe mangos (or
peaches)
¼ cup honey, preferably
tangerine
¼ cup raspberry wine vinegar
½ teaspoon orange extract

2 tablespoons mango or
peach jam
¼ teaspoon cinnamon
1 teaspoon granulated sugar
¼ cup extra virgin olive oil
Salt and pepper to taste
1 large ripe mango or peach

1. Combine ingredients several hours in advance, reserving the last mango or peach.

2. Directly before serving, chop or slice the mango or peach and add. Microwave 1 minute. Spoon over grilled pork.

Individual Chocolate Soufflés
6 Individual soufflés made without flour

4 ounces good quality semi-sweet chocolate
½ cup heavy cream
3 jumbo egg yolks
1 tablespoon vanilla extract
5 jumbo egg whites brought to room temperature or warmer

¼ teaspoon cream of tartar
Pinch of salt
⅓ cup granulated sugar
Confectioner's 10X sugar for dusting
Soufflé dishes that hold ¾ cup liquid (6 ounces)

In Advance:
1. Melt the chocolate and cream over low heat. When chocolate is soft, stir well with a wooden spoon and then a wire whisk until smooth and thick. Add the vanilla and stir again.
2. Pour a little of the chocolate mixture into the egg yolks and stir. Add to the chocolate in the pot and cook, stirring, over low heat until very thick. Remove from the heat and cover tightly.
3. Rub softened unsalted butter over the bottom and around the sides of the soufflé dishes. Sprinkle a little sugar into the dishes and tip around to coat the sides. (over the sink) Tip out any excess.

To Cook and Serve:
1. Pre-heat oven to 425°F and set rack on lowest level

2. Beat egg whites on highest speed of an electric mixer until foamy. Add the cream of tartar and continue to beat until very thick. Sprinkle in the sugar and beat until very thick and smooth. (About 10 seconds)
3. Fold ½ of the whites into the chocolate mixture. Fold in the other half and spoon immediately into the soufflé dishes, running your finger around the inside rim of each. Heap a little more soufflé in the center to create a mound and put immediately in the oven.
4. Bake 6 minutes. Reduce oven temperature to 400°F and bake for another 2 ½ minutes. Remove from the oven. Sprinkle lightly with sifted powdered sugar and serve immediately.

Note: Do not allow soufflé to stand after folding in the whites. Bake and serve immediately.

A triangular piece of white chocolate may be inserted into the center of the soufflé just before placing in the oven. It's just another fun presentation.

Vanilla Sauce
Yield: Approximately 2 cups

4 jumbo egg yolks
1 cup fat-free half & half
1 cup heavy cream
½ cup (scant) granulated sugar

1 tablespoon vanilla extract
(Optional: 2 tablespoons Kahlua, Frangelico, or Grand Marnier liqueur)

1. Separate the eggs, placing the yolks into a small bowl or cup. Save the whites in an air- tight container in the refrigerator for meringue cookies. Or, save 2 whites for

Chocolate Soufflé without Flour that calls for 3 yolks and 5 egg whites.

2. Combine the half & half, cream, and sugar in a saucepan and cook, stirring, over medium heat until sugar is dissolved and mixture is hot.

3. Stir approximately ½ cup into the yolks. Pour the mixture through a strainer into the saucepan. (Adding a bit of the hot mixture to the yolks will keep the yolks from curdling when being stirred into the pot. Straining will insure a smooth sauce).

4. Stir in vanilla and liqueur. Cook over medium heat, stirring constantly with a stainless spoon for 7-8 minutes, or until mixture begins to thicken ever so slightly and reaches 160°F when a thermometer is inserted into the center. Do not allow mixture to boil or it will curdle. When a thin layer adheres to the spoon, the sauce is done.

5. Cool to room temperature. Refrigerate at least 24 hours for the flavors to settle and thicken. The sauce will last, refrigerated, for 4 days. Serve in a sauceboat to accompany any soufflé or with fresh berries.

Note: This recipe is more difficult than it appears. A few seconds can make the difference between a beautiful sauce and a curdled disaster. The sauce does not become thick. It changes consistency.

So-Be Hot Brownies
Yield 9X9 inch pan

5 ounces unsweetened chocolate

1 full tablespoon vanilla extract

1 tablespoon Frangelico liqueur or ½ teaspoon hazelnut extract

½ cup butter

½ cup vegetable oil

4 jumbo eggs

2 ½ cups granulated sugar

1 cup all-purpose flour, sifted with

1 full tablespoon unsweetened cocoa

½ teaspoon salt

1. Preheat oven to 350ºF.
2. Rub vegetable oil on the bottom and sides of the pan.
3. Combine the chocolate, vanilla, liqueur (or extract), butter and oil in a saucepan and place over very low heat until the chocolate melts. Do not stir.
4. Combine the eggs and sugar in a bowl and beat until light and creamy in texture.
5. Sift the flour with the cocoa and salt and add to the batter.
6. Bake 35-40 minutes, or until a wood pick inserted in the center is encrusted in chocolate but not liquid. Do not over-bake.

Serve with a scoop of vanilla ice cream.

These can also be rewarmed in the microwave 15 seconds.

These brownies freeze beautifully. Defrost and microwave to heat.

"Your life does not get better by chance, it gets better by change."
— Jim Rohn

Changing Direction

THE BRASS BOX WITH SAM'S ashes sits on top of dad's desk in his office. He stares at the inscription, SAM BEAR, 1975-1991. Sixteen years had gone by too quickly. His car is empty without his friend next to him regally posed for other motorists to admire. His employees no longer greet the pair at the door to say good morning to Sam and be rewarded with his undivided attention. He reaches under his desk, expecting to touch the big head and finds emptiness. He no longer feels any enthusiasm for the business he loved. The children have moved away to pursue their own careers instead of joining his. The lifetime he spent building his success seems wasted because no one is interested in its continuation. Like a king sitting on the throne without an heir, he is lonely and alone. As the months pass he becomes increasingly discontented. One morning, while going through his mail, he sees an advertisement for country homes. Everyone else has moved on. It is time for him to do the same.

Someone told us about a charming little Victorian town in the center of Florida, an hour northwest of Disney World. One Saturday morning in July we followed the Turnpike until we saw the sign leading us to Mount Dora. A local realtor helped us explore the rural community and surrounding farmlands.

Peace of mind is the entity humans have strived to find since the beginning of time. Sadly, most never change direction of their motion or mindset to allow them to find the magnetic field that produces the force that will change their lives. We found ourselves entering into this field and reached out to grasp the magical moment. The big house was set deep into a forest of live oak trees. Next to it was an open field blanketed with myriad colors from thousands of wild flowers that had once been a flourishing citrus grove before the great freeze of the 1980s. How lovely it would be to have a weekend getaway in the country. Sunday afternoon the house and field were ours.

"A cat's eyes are windows enabling us to see into another world."
— Irish Legend

Commuting

Every Thursday afternoon we drove to Mount Dora where carpenters and painters were busily turning the unfinished house into a designer's dream. It took almost a year to rebuild the kitchen, add bathrooms and closets and install new carpet, wallpaper and curtains. When the workmen finally finished, we decided we were meant to live in the country. We sold the house where I lived with Sam, called a moving company to take all our furniture up to Mount Dora, and purchased a small apartment overlooking the Atlantic Ocean on Miami Beach that was big enough for just the three of us. Because I missed sleeping with Sam, I was given permission to spend nights at the foot of their bed. After they fell asleep, I quietly tiptoed across the covers to snuggle against *mom's* legs. She must have known I was there, but never pushed me away. Sometimes I became a bit too brazen and moved upward, resting my head against her neck so I could hear her heartbeat like my mama's and Sam's. Several times I even snuck into her hair on the pillow. It wasn't as long and thick as I remembered Susan's, but it was soft and snuggly.

As the months went by, our travel pattern changed. We were now spending weekends in Miami Beach and weekdays in the country. I loved commuting. I slept in-between *mom* and *dad* on the front seat of the station wagon and they shared their ham and chicken and tuna sandwiches with me during the four and a half hour drive. When we arrived at the underground garage of the apartment building in Miami Beach, they carried me into the elevator. As soon as the door closed, they put me down. I counted slowly to three, which was the time it took to reach the third floor. The minute the elevator stopped and the doors opened I ran down the hallway to the door I knew was ours and pawed at it to get in. Then I ran over to the window and jumped up to the sill. It wasn't deep enough to sleep on, so I sat erect with my front paws together in show stance as is my custom. I could sit for hours, watching the distant ships in the ocean, wondering what it was like to have been a cat that protected an ancient vessel, bringing good fortune and ensuring the safety of the sailors aboard. I might have been a cat on one of the Phoenician cargo ships that brought the first domesticated cats to Europe in 900 BC. On second thought, I surely would have been the charmed Manx cat. Superstitious sailors in the olden days believed that cats stored magic in their tails that could bring on a storm. Because the Manx had no tail it brought good luck only. I could have even been aboard one of the ships of the Spanish Armada wrecked in 1588 off the Isle of Man in the Irish Sea between England and Ireland. I would have swam ashore and lived in a paradise among thousands of tiny fat succulently sweet mice on that beautiful rustic island. Then again, suppose I didn't swim to shore from the sunken ship, but was the Cymric long-haired version of the Manx, brought to the Isle of Man by the Vikings. Since Welsh folklore considered all tailless cats sacred, either specie would have suited me just fine.

Still sitting in an erect position with my head up and front legs together, I begin to feel my eyelids closing into narrow slits like a near-sighted person attempting to make out images too far in the distance to perceive..... . I was drifting into history......

"Then three times 'round went our gallant ship,
And three times 'round went she,
And the third time that she went 'round
She sank to the bottom of the sea."
— <u>The Mermaid Song</u>, Francis J. Child 1825-1826

The Spanish
Armada 1588

Lisbon, Spain – My Great Moment

"Ahoy Mates! No one boards the ships until we bring the cats. Now step back and make way for our lucky four- legged felines."

Twenty-two great fighting galleons from Spain and Portugal await their signals for departure. Behind them stands a fleet of merchant ships converted for battle and several dozen smaller ships that will be employed as messengers and guard duty. Huge, ungainly looking "urca" transport ships are being loaded from bow to stern with surplus guns and ammunition as well as horses and mules for the projected land battles. Accompanying the sailors will be physicians and surgeons as well as almost two hundred priests and spiritual advisors. Twenty honored judges and fifty administrators have been selected for the voyage to set up the new government in England. Enough food will be stocked for the thirty thousand men who will call the one hundred thirty sailing ships their home for the next six months. Eleven thousand pounds of sweet bread known as hardtack or ship's biscuit, six hundred pounds salt pork, forty thousand gallons olive oil, and fourteen thousand barrels of wine are but a few of the provisions being loaded. Thousands of extra shoes and clothing will also be stored, as well as equipment to repair the ships and tools for the land battles after they reach shore. Our masterful King, Philip II, has readied this great fleet to sail north through the English channel where we will meet with the Duke of Parma's army of the Spanish Netherlands and accompany them to the shores of England. Together they will have enough power to match the English at sea and invade English soil.

We believe that Philip is the rightful King of England to succeed Mary, the Catholic Queen of Scotland, who proclaimed him as such before she was executed by the Protestant, Queen Elizabeth 1st of England, last year. When this takes place, Catholicism will be restored and Spain will rule the world.

A parade of proud sailors carrying cages walk single file up the ramps of each of the ships waiting to set sail. There are two cats in each cage. Each vessel will have several dozen prized cats on board to insure protection from the mermaids and monsters that live within the depths of the sea and the dreaded diseases that lurk within the darkness of the ship's bowels.

I am the first to be carried up the gangway of one of the head command ships reserved for the most able and bravest seamen of Spain. I sit erect in my cage, aware that hundreds of eyes are focused on me. I have been carefully chosen because I am a member of the unique breed of shorthaired cats born without a tail. Although I am of medium size, my overall appearance is round from my head to my chest and rump. My muzzle is actually slightly longer than the top part of my head, giving credibility to large round whisker pads that jut out from my prominent cheek bones and wide jowls. My ears are also more distinctive than cats of a lesser lineage. They flare out so wide apart that when viewed from behind, they resemble the keel of a ship or rockers on the bottom of a baby's crib. Within my round exterior is firm, dense muscle, giving my body the impression of a baby bear with no tail. It is said that I resemble a rabbit rather than a bear when I am running possibly because my hind legs are slightly higher than my front legs. The absence of a tail is an absolute necessity. The practical and superstitious bond that sailors have had with cats since ancient Egyptian history has taken on a new dimension in present times. Sailors have always believed that cats could start storms through magic stored in their tails if they became agitated. Many sailors will not touch or even look at the cats they have on board for fear of incurring their wrath. A cat without a tail insures a safe journey without dangerous storms. Sailors have been cautiously warned to protect their cats and never inflict injury on them even if such an act is justifiable.

Rigorous training that began last year confined us to dark dungeons with dangerous criminals. Our mission to seek and destroy the vermin that lived unabashed within the entrails of that horrific environment was to prepare us for our long journey. Now, many months later on this beautiful warm afternoon in 1588, we are finally boarding the great Armada to perform our duties with the expertise of true professionals.

Cheers from the crowd confirm I am indeed a charmed member of the tailless breed that will cease ill winds from destroying the gallant ships of the Spanish Armada. I and my compatriots will conquer England and reign supreme in trade and power over land and sea. Never again will English pirates like Sir Francis Drake attack our Spanish treasure ships and steal our silver. I take a brief glance at my partner in the cage, making sure not to move any part of my body. He is sitting as erect as I, with his head high and his gaze fixed straight ahead in anticipation of boarding.

The minute our cages touch the deck, they are opened. Our great Navy of cats explodes forth in perfect formation toward the cargo hatch where we disappear into the inside of the hull, known as the hold of the ship.

I command my crew to remain absolutely still because the crowd is now cheering our Captain, Medina Sidonia. We are ready to begin our journey.

English Channel - The Defeat

The voyage north has been quite lovely. The seas have been calm but for a few days of scattered gales, and the sailors are content. I'm not sure how long we have been at sea but my instinctual barometer has begun to fluctuate, indicating that summer is coming to an end and the changing currants will soon be bringing in September storms.

At the moment we are anchored off France near the port of Calais. Under normal circumstances we could reach the vicinity of Parma's troops sometime tomorrow, but my messengers tell me there might be a problem because the size of our cortege makes harboring in a single port impossible. If we wait for Parma to muster his forces from their scattered positions in the Dutch canal system, we will surely be sitting ducks, an easy target for the English to attack.

Then just before midnight, the smell of fire and gunpowder begins to seep into our stations under the decks in the ship's hold. Later we would know this was the famous English nighttime "dispatch of the fireships" in which Drake set fire to old hulks laden with pitch and gunpowder and sent them in our direction. But, the sailors do not know this is a prank to scare us away and they begin to panic. I hear Captain Sidonia bellowing from the lead ship to cut anchor and turn around to escape out of range and regroup into battle formation.

The hours that follow are a blur of noise and destruction. Our hulls and masts are repeatedly battered by the rapid fire of the English canons with us not able to retaliate in full force because many of the cannonballs that were loaded on our ships do not match the size of our guns. The only reason our ships are not breaking up and sinking is because the English have run out of ammunition. It will become known as the Battle of Gravelines, to be remembered until eternity. After months of anticipating victory, the battle has finished before it began. And now, Captain Sidonia is instructing his ships to let the northerly winds carry them toward the Netherlands and around the tip of Scotland in order to sail southward in the Atlantic to return to Spain and Portugal.

The Spanish Armada 1588

"I am a creature of the Fey
Prepare to give your soul away
My spell is passion and it is art
My song can bind a human heart
And if you chance to know my face
My hold shall be your last embrace"
— <u>Creature of the Wood</u>, Bard Heather Alexander

Storm and Salvation

The storm began off the west coast of Ireland, passed over Orkney and then funneled down the North Sea and Northern Atlantic, driving a deadly mountain of water before it. At first it was only a moderate disturbance and we sailed safely through the Fair Isle Channel between the Shetland and Orkney Islands in the Norwegian Sea. But most of the ships are leaking water from direct hits by the English. Our food supplies are at a dangerous low and the men are tired and sick. The morale of the crew is diminishing hourly and the winds are becoming increasing violent. We know of eight galleons that have already sunk and we have lost sight of many of the others. We can only hope and pray they are finding their way safely to land, but know the reality is that their inevitable fate will be to break up from the wrathful gales or crash onto the rocks and sink as they attempt to go around the northern coasts of Scotland and Ireland.

We tailless cats in the hold anticipate the disaster. We know this will be one of the worst September storms recorded in history. It is not our fault. We did not bring this terrible tragedy to the Armada. But we cannot ward it off no matter how hard we try. The Armada will be destroyed because of the stupidity of one of the sailors.

He was a young man and this was his first voyage. Without

223

proper training, naive and ill-experienced, he was a perfect victim. One night while on watch on the upper deck, he saw a mermaid beckoning to him from the sea. She was exquisite to behold. Her voluptuous body that was naked to the waist rose above the surface of the waves. She had long blond, silken hair that she was combing with one hand while holding a golden mirror in the other. The sound of her voice was the most beautiful song he had ever heard. It beckoned him to abandon all his earthly troubles and give his body and soul completely to her. No longer would he be hungry or thirsty or frightened. She would love and protect him forever in the depths of her water home. He dove in after her and drowned. His friend came on deck at the very moment he was being taken under the water by the deadly siren. He turned and spotted one of my messengers lurking in the shadows. In his fright and fury he grabbed the cat by its neck and flung it overboard. Several members of the crew witnessed this horrific brutality and immediately fastened irons to his wrists and legs. Everyone knew it was forbidden to commit any offense against a ship's cat. To purposefully murder a cat held the penalty of death. Bad luck would follow his blasphemous deed. The ship would be doomed.

The trial lasted but a few minutes. First they prayed, not for the accused but for their ship that had already begun to take on water. Then they bound his arms and legs with rope and heaved him into the sea to join his irresponsible friend.

Within a few hours, the squalls from gale force winds and blinding rain raging through the Northern Atlantic and North Seas begin to wrench us in all directions. We have lost contact with the other vessels and we cannot direct ours. As the storm continues to worsen and the ship pitches and rocks, the enormous masts break off and huge pieces of the sidings splinter into the ocean. Water is gushing into the hold we once considered the safest part of our home at sea. In the distance I can hear the high whirling sing of a cyclone and I know it is coming toward us and we cannot get out of its path.

Hear me mates, and get thee to the bulkhead at the bow of the ship. It's our only hope for survival.

A cacophony of discordant noise shatters our ear drums as we are struck full force by the cyclone. As it encircles us and the ship swirls in disorientation, we are thrown through the darkness, our bodies dashing against the hard planks.

Mayday, Mayday, I cry through the noise of the fury, *it's every feline for itself. Hold onto the boards. Do not attempt to swim or you will surely drown.*

I dig my claws into a thick piece of wood just as an enormous explosion blows the ship apart. Hanging on with all my might, I fly with it through the air and then down a zillion miles into the cold depths of the angry Irish Sea. The second I open my eyes I grasp the wood more tightly, pulling myself onto it while holding on for dear life. I realize I am not on a single board but a large piece of the bulkhead. Some of my mates are next to me, most of them too scared and shaken from the blast and fall to comprehend what has happened.

Many hours pass before the storm subsides. The currant is still strong, carrying my strange vessel swiftly to the northwest, but the waters that splash over my body have become decidedly warmer. A quick calculation tells me we have drifted into the Gulf Stream. And then, I see the sun beginning to rise magnificently from the east horizon.

My Best Life

Land, I meow weakly, *land, I see land!*

The coast is dangerously rocky. It will take strength and courage for the tired cats to make their way to safety but I have confidence.

Paddle on my brave mates, paddle on!

We swim to the rocks and then crawl up and around to a land of green pasture abundantly bearing fruits, vegetables, and grains. Cows and sheep graze contentedly and the aroma of thousands of tiny, succulent field mice envelops my entire being. We have come ashore halfway between England and Ireland on the Isle of Man, a tiny fertile little slice of heaven. This craggy shoreline near Port Erin and Castletown will become known to the world as Spanish Point.

The little survivors of the Spanish Armada's navy scamper around the lush pastures with renewed exuberance. I do not see the two long-haired cats approaching until they are upon me. They are incredibly beautiful, statuesque and regal of stance, allowing no question of their royal heritage. Both have heavy, glossy double coats with white chests and white markings on their faces, but one has jet black hair over the rest of its body, while the other is chestnut brown. I look again in complete shock. Their bodies are shaped exactly like ours and they are tailless. They have no tails, just like us.

Where have you come from, they ask?

I tell them everything before asking the same question while exclaiming my surprise how similar they are to us.

We could be of the same unique bloodline. Are you originally Spanish, I ask?

We do not know. Our ancestors have been on the Isle of Man forever. Some say we were brought here by Phoenician sailors before the Common Era. We are the Cymric cats. We pronounce it Kumrc' or Koom rik. The name came from Cymru, the ancient Welsh word for Wales. We are pure Welsh and the symbol of The Isle of Man. We welcome you who have arrived on the ship from Spain as our short-haired cousins. I will baptize you 'Manx' after the ancient language and people of our island.

Pondering his words, I settle onto my side and lick the salt water from my paws.

What is a Manx and what is your language and who are your people?

Our people are called Manx because it is the language we speak and our cultural heritage. The language is an offshoot of Irish but it is closely related to the eastern dialects of Irish and Scottish. It is also called Gaelic and Goidelig or Gaelg in Manx, which means that it has some of all the insular Celtic languages that include Irish Gaelic, Scottish Gaelic and Manx. The Manx language also has many Old Norse words that became part of it when the Vikings raided the island during the ninth and tenth centuries. They were originally a bad group of savage pirates who murdered without conscience and stole anything they wanted. In 1079, we were conquered by their leader, Godred Crovan. He ruled us for sixteen years. When a large number of his warriors decided to remain with him, they brought their language and customs. They also abolished their worship of many gods and became good Christians and upstanding citizens. They married with our people and the island enjoyed peace and tranquility that still exists today. It is said that he established our Manx Parliament with their Norse tradition of an open-air assembly of members called a Tynwald. Their language became so intertwined with ours that, after a while, it was all one. Our Manx language is spoken only on the Isle of Man. We are a most unique island, fertile and happy, with our peace-loving humans and exquisite Cymric cats. Because of your bravery and loyalty to Philip, You bring pride and good fortune to all of us. Your descendants will be known as the charmed tailless Manx. We welcome you to our land.

Garlic Soup

The poor farmers' staple that became a gourmet specialty
Yield: Approximately 6 cups

6 cups water
4-5 garlic cloves, minced
2 tablespoons Spanish
  olive oil
6 thin slices day old bread
  with crusts (French or
  whole grain)

2 teaspoons Hungarian sweet
  paprika
1 teaspoon salt
¼ teaspoon rosemary or 1
  small sprig fresh
¼ teaspoon ground thyme, or
  more to taste
4 jumbo eggs

1. Combine water and garlic in a pot. Boil gently 5 minutes.
2. Heat the oil in a skillet with the paprika, salt, rosemary, and thyme. Set the bread slices in and brown on both sides.
3. Add the bread to the soup pot to cook over very low heat 10 minutes.
4. Remove from the heat and let it stand several hours.
5. Directly before serving, break the eggs, one at a time, into a soup ladle. Stir to break the yolks before dropping into the soup.
6. Stir and serve immediately.

Spanish Lobster with Spicy Tomato Sauce
(Langosta Salsa De Tomate Picante)
Yield: 2 servings

Spiny Lobster: 2 pounds raw lobster = 10.6 ounces meat
Maine lobster 3 pound = 10 ounces meat

2 pound Florida or California
Spiny lobster (no claws) or
3 pound Maine lobster
1 onion, chopped fine but not
minced
2 ribs celery, chopped fine but
not minced
¼ pound baby bella (Crimini)
mushrooms, sliced thin

2-3 cloves garlic, minced
½ cup extra virgin olive oil
8 ounces Chorizo sausage (or
hot Italian), sliced thin
2-15 ounce cans tomatoes
with chili peppers or
Mexican spices

1. Bring a large pot of water to a boil. Drop the lobster in and cook, covered, at a full boil 10 minutes. Remove from the water to cool.
2. Combine the onion, celery, mushrooms, garlic and sausage with the oil in a deep skillet. Cook over low heat until vegetables are soft, turning often.
3. Discard all but ¼ cup of the water in the canned tomatoes. Cut tomatoes into small pieces and stir into the vegetables Taste for seasoning to add a touch of white pepper or cayenne. Remove from the heat.
4. Remove the lobster from its shell and cut into large bite-size pieces. Stir into the vegetable mixture.
5. Directly before serving, bring the lobster and vegetables to a boil, stirring constantly.
6. Serve over rice or pasta.

Paella from the Sea
Yield: Approximately 6 servings

2-1¼ pound lobsters, body removed - claws cracked, tails cut crosswise into 1-inch pieces
36 large shrimp (U21-25)
18 large mussels, well-scrubbed, beards removed
24 littleneck clams, well-scrubbed
1 pound chorizo or mild Italian sausage
½ cup Spanish olive oil

2 large onions, chopped coarse
2 garlic cloves, minced
1 teaspoon saffron threads or 1 envelope saffron powder
½ teaspoon crushed hot red pepper, or to taste
24 ounces crushed canned tomatoes
2 cups clam juice
2 cups long grain rice
15 ounce can baby peas, drained

1. Plunge the tip of a large sharp knife into the soft opening between the eyes of the lobsters to kill them instantly. Cut downward into the body to reveal the tomalley and eggs. Remove the tomalley and eggs. Remove and crack the claws. Cut the tails crosswise into 1-inch pieces. Set aside.
2. Remove the shells from the shrimp. Remove the dark vein along the backs. Set aside.
3. Scrub the mussels and clams. Set aside.
4. Preheat the oven to 350ºF. Set the chorizo on aluminum foil and cook 10 minutes or until browned. Cool and slice into rounds approximately ½ inch.
5. In a large deep skillet or paella pan set over low heat cook the onions and garlic in the olive oil until soft but not colored. Add saffron, red pepper, canned tomatoes, and clam juice.

6. Add the rice and reserved lobsters, shrimp, mussels and clams. Bring to a boil. Cover the pan. Reduce heat to low. Add the sliced sausage. Cook 10-12 minutes, or until the rice is soft, the lobsters cooked, and the clams and mussels have opened.
7. Cover the top with peas. Place the cover on the pan for the peas to become hot.
8. Bring the pan to the table to serve.

Armada's Last Land Meal
Pork Chops Sautéed with Sausage and Apples
(Cerdo con Chorizo y Manzanas)
Yield: 4 servings

4 pork rib chops, ¾-1 inch thick, fat removed
Salt, pepper
Flour to dust
Spanish extra virgin olive oil just to cover the bottom of a small non-stick deep skillet
1-2 cloves garlic, crushed
1 small purple onion, sliced thin
1 large apple (preferably Fiji or Honeycrisp), peeled and sliced

½ pound or more chorizo Spanish cooked sausage (Pepperoni or Kielbasa can be substituted)
1 cup apple juice
1 cup chicken broth
1cup pink kidney or white cannelloni beans, drained if canned, or soaked 4 hours in hot water.

1. Rinse and dry pork chops. With a sharp knife, remove fat from edges. Sprinkle with salt and pepper. Dust with flour.

2. Cover the bottom of a small deep skillet with olive oil. Cook the chops very quickly over high heat to brown on both sides. Remove from the skillet.
3. Reduce the heat to simmer and add the garlic, onion, apple slices, and chorizo.
4. Stir in the apple juice and chicken broth. Cover the pan and cook all very slowly, stirring occasionally, for 30 minutes.
5. Remove chops to individual plates or platter. Stir the beans into the sauce and spoon over to serve.

Ship's Sweet Bread
Yield: Approximately 24 rolls

1 package dry yeast (¼ ounce)
1 tablespoon granulated sugar
¼ cup lukewarm water
1 cup lukewarm milk
¼ pound unsalted butter
⅓ cup granulated sugar

1 jumbo or 2 extra large egg
  yolks
½ teaspoon vanilla extract
3 cups bread flour mixed with
  ½ teaspoon salt
Cupcake pans

1. Sprinkle the yeast and sugar over the lukewarm water and stir until dissolved.(Make sure the temperature is just lukewarm (100°F.). If too cool, the yeast will not grow, if too hot, it will kill the yeast.
2. Allow mixture to sit 10 minutes.
3. Beat the butter and sugar until thick and lemon-colored. Add the egg yolk(s). Add the vanilla.
4. Beat in the flour and yeast mixture with a heavy wood spoon or on the lowest speed of an electric mixer fitted with a bread hook attachment. Roll into a loose ball. Cover with

a damp towel and allow it to rise in a warm place for 1 ½ hours, or until doubled in bulk.

Filling

4 tablespoons melted butter
¼ cup cinnamon/sugar (1 part cinnamon to 7 parts granulated sugar)

½ cup chopped pecans
Optional: 4 ounces golden raisins or dried cranberries

1. Sprinkle the risen dough with flour and push it flat. Divide into 2 pieces. Set the pieces on a floured surface. Sprinkle the tops with flour and work each with your hands - push, turn, flatten – at least 4 times. (kneading the dough) Roll the dough to flatten to ⅛-inch thick rectangles.
2. Brush each rectangle with melted butter. Sprinkle with cinnamon/sugar. Sprinkle the pecans and raisins over. Roll up lengthwise as a jelly roll.

To Finish

¼ pound unsalted melted butter
2 tablespoons water

¾ cup dark brown sugar
¾ cup light brown sugar

1. Melt the butter with the water. Stir in the sugars. Spoon a tablespoon into each cupcake holder.
2. Slice the dough into pieces ½-inch thick and place flat into the cups to show the spiral. Cover with damp dish towels to rise 15 minutes.

3. Preheat oven to 375°F.
4. Place rolls one-third from the bottom of the oven and immediately reduce the heat to 350°F. Bake 20 minutes or until golden brown. Turn upside down immediately on to parchment or wax paper.

The Perfect Spanish Flan
Yield: 6 servings

½ cup granulated sugar
3 tablespoons water

6 ramekins or soufflé dishes
to hold ½ cup liquid

1-inch piece vanilla bean, split
1 cinnamon stick, broken in half
½ cup granulated sugar

2 cups fat-free half & half
1 whole jumbo egg
3 jumbo egg yolks
Pinch of salt

1. Preheat oven to 350°F.
2. Combine ½ cup sugar with 3 tablespoons water in a saucepan. Stir sugar to dissolve over low heat. Bring to a boil and cook without stirring until sugar turns light brown. Watch carefully so it does not burn.
3. Remove from heat and pour into 6 ramekins or soufflé dishes.
4. Wash saucepan.
5. Combine vanilla, cinnamon, and ½ cup sugar in the saucepan. Stir in milk. Over very low heat, let mixture stand 10 minutes.
6. Raise heat for milk to simmer slowly. Do not allow it to boil.

7. With a wire whisk, beat the egg and yolks in a bowl until frothy. Slowly whisk in the milk. Pour into the ramekins.
8. Set ramekins into a dish with 1 inch water to come up the sides of the ramekins.
9. Bake 45 minutes. Cool. Refrigerate.
10. Invert ramekins on to separate dishes to serve with whipped cream or fruit.

"Genteel in personage, conduct, and equipage;
Noble by heritage, generous and free."
— <u>The Contrivances,</u> Act 1, Henry Carey, 1663-1743

"A cat's eyes are windows enabling us to see into another world."
— Irish Legend

Our Scottish Neighbors

SOMEWHERE IN THE BACK OF my dream I hear
something that sounds like a meow. Yes, it is definitely a meow.
In fact, there seems to be two meows. And they are distinctly
different from each other. I take one last look at the ships in
the ocean before jumping down from the window sill to strut in
the direction of the front door from where the sounds seem to
be coming. Fortunately, it had been left open to cross circulate
the air from the hallway to the apartment. The door across
the hall is also open. I peek into the foyer and meow, *is anyone
home?* Two of the funniest looking cats I have ever seen are
sleeping flat on their backs next to each other on a sofa. They
are short and pudgy and completely round. Even their huge,
fluffy tails are 'roly-poly' round. Both have semi-longish hair
that has been perfectly brushed as though they were about to
enter the center ring to compete in a cat show. The bigger one is
sort of yellowish in color with a fluffy mound of soft white chest
hair and a white fluff at the tip of its tail, while the other has
black fur covering its eyes and cheeks with a white formation
that begins at the top of its head and forms a perfect triangle
across its nose and mouth and half of its cheeks. The rest of its
body, including its paws, is covered with pure white fur except
for another enormous round black patch on its back and a jet
black tail. It kind of resembles the tuxedo *dad* wears to formal
parties. I take another look and gasp. The white and black one
has the strangest ears. They are tiny and tightly folded in three

238

places, making it seem as though it has no ears at all. The other has ears that stand straight up. With the exception of their coloration and ears, their faces and bodies are identical. Their eyes are large, round, and broadly spaced. Their noses are short and wide to match the wide set of their eyes, and the curve of their mouths around their prominent whisker pads make them look as though they are smiling at me.

They were indeed smiling at me. *Welcome to our home,* they say in unison with a strange musical inflection of the first three words, *welcome to our,* before ending with *hooome* that sings straight up into the air almost as a question rather than a statement. It is the cutest accent for the cutest cats and I am absolutely taken in.

> *Thank you. You're a very lovely looking twosome.*
> *My name is Sakie. Do you have names?*

The yellow boy that is the larger of the two sings first.

> *My name is Colin. It's Scottish. Some say it means, 'hound' but others claim it means 'virile'. It's considered to be Biblical because there were a number of saints who carried the name.*

Then, the tuxedo with the funny ears lifts its head to chant in the same up and down melody,

> *I am Heather. I am named for the small, low lying green shrub with the flower of tiny petals, some purple and some white, that grow upon the hillsides of Scotland to make them more beautiful. The heather can grow in even the poorest soil and*

239

*withstand the wind and the rain and the cold. It is
renowned for three God given gifts: The bark is the
strongest of any tree or shrub in the whole world.
The flower has the fragrance of honeysuckle used to
create perfume. And, it has the sweetness of the rose,
making it the favorite flower of the bee to pollinate.*

She was not bragging but merely stating a fact. She is truly
beautiful and definitely sweet, and I am duly impressed.
And, then again, lilting in unison:

*We are the Scottish Fold cat. We were discovered in
1961 in the Tayside Region of a Scottish farm near
Coupar Angus. The original one had only a single,
or loose, fold where the tips of her ears bent forward
about halfway up the ear. British geneticists mated
her with a cat with straight ears to create the triple
fold. It seems as though when a kitten that inherits
a gene from one parent for straight ears and one
from a parent with the gene for folded ears are
mated, they will produce a triple fold in the next
generation. Some Scottish Fold cats still have a loose
single fold, but the ears of show cats you see in the
ring are all triple fold.*

Do you have a mate, they ask?

*No. I just have my people family. I had a dog named
Sam. He was my best friend but he died.*

How sad, they say, looking genuinely sorry for
me. *You must be very lonely. Even though we love*

*our people, we do not know what we would do
without each other.*

I could not tell them that I am perfectly content being
alone. I do not think I would want another cat sharing my litter
box or water bowl. Before turning to leave, I raise my paw in
my signature Japanese Bobtail greeting and say, *I am happy to
have met you both. I hope to see you again.*

As I round the corner to exit through their front door I turn
my head for a last glance. They have already forgotten me and
are curled up next to each other about to turn over again onto
their backs for another nap.

A Feast for Scottish Fold Twins
Baked Trout in Vermouth
Yield: 4 servings

4 Rainbow Trout, 8 ounces or
larger, well cleaned inside –
scales and fins removed
⅓ cup dry vermouth
Sprinkling of salt
Sprinkling of black pepper
4 pieces parchment paper

Olive oil to brush the foil
4 teaspoons unsalted butter,
melted
Handful of fresh dill,
chopped scallion greens,
and parsley

1. Preheat oven to 425°F.
2. Cut 4 pieces of parchment paper large enough to fold over
    each fish
3. Brush the surface of the paper with olive oil and set a fish
    in the center.

4. Sprinkle the inside of the fish with salt and pepper. Brush with butter. Insert the dill, scallion greens, and parsley.
5. Close the fish and brush vermouth on both sides.
6. Fold the paper over the fish, sides and ends to create a closed box.
7. Bake 8-10 minutes, or until white without any pink or opaque (dull color).
8. Serve with boiled potatoes and a green vegetable.

Scottish Song Shrimp
Prawns in Whiskey Cream
Yield: 4 servings

16 prawns (jumbo shrimp U16-20 to the pound), shelled, deveined, tails left on
4 individual baking dishes or 1 shallow casserole dish
Melted unsalted butter to brush the bottom of the dish(es)
4 tablespoons unsalted butter

1 sweet onion, minced
¾ cup heavy cream
3 tablespoons light Scotch whiskey (Dewar's White Label®, if available)
Salt and pepper to taste
½ cup grated Beaufort or Gruyère cheese
Parsley to garnish

1. Brush the baking dish(es) with butter.
2. Sauté the onion in 4 tablespoons butter until just soft. Add the prawns and heat on both sides.
3. Stir in the Scotch and bring to a boil.
4. Remove from the heat and stir in the cream. Reduce the heat to low and return the pan to warm the cream, stirring constantly.

5. Sprinkle in salt and pepper to taste.
6. Divide among the dishes or arrange in the casserole.
7. Sprinkle the cheese over the top and place under the broiler to brown. Decorate with parsley.

Cock-A-Leekie Soup – Reduced Fat
(A cock is a young male chicken)
Yield: Approximately 14 cups

6-8 pound chicken or 2
   chickens weighing 4
   pounds each
6 leeks, white part only
2 large white onions, peeled
   and cut into quarters
Optional: 2 cloves garlic,
   peeled and split
Bottom of whole celery plus 2
   ribs, cut up
2 whole cloves
1 bunch parsley

1 bunch dill weed
2 teaspoons kosher or coarse
   sea salt
1 teaspoon black pepper
5 quarts cool water
4-5 carrots, sliced and cubed
⅓ cup quick cooking barley
New potatoes, cooked and
   sliced
Optional: 4 ounces cooked,
   pitted prunes

1. Remove the skin from the chicken. Remove as much fat as possible. If necessary, cut the chicken in half or quarters to fit into your soup pot.
2. Preheat oven to 375°F.
3. Place the white part of the leeks on aluminum foil and roast until they turn color, approximately twenty minutes.
4. Combine the leek with remaining ingredients in a large pot, reserving the carrots for later. Skim off any dark froth that

bubbles on top. Cover. Reduce heat to medium and boil gently for 1½ hours. Remove the chicken.

5. Cool the soup stock to room temperature. Strain. Remove the meat from its bones. Refrigerate the soup stock and chicken meat separately.

6. Return the soup to the soup pot.

7. Add the carrots and bring the soup to a boil. Stir in the barley or rice. Boil gently until the barley is soft, approximately 20 minutes. Stir in the prunes. Stir in the sliced potatoes.

8. Cut the chicken into bite-size pieces and add to the soup. Correct the seasoning and serve.

"Ye've got to love each brick an' stone from cellar up t' dome;
It takes a heap o' livin' in a house t' make it home."
— Edgar Guest, <u>A Heap of Living,</u> 1916

Chain of Lakes

I HAVE FOUND THE PERFECT NAPPING place in our country home where the morning sun creates a path through the glass doors that open to the woods. Birds of all sizes and colors explore the branches, singing happily. Butterflies kiss the flowers. And squirrels play tag with each other around the trees. Somewhere in the distance a hawk screeches. There are two eagles that have built a nest on top of the tallest tree in the very back of the woods. They say there is a second nest overlooking Lake Beauclair a half mile away. Eagles always have two nests in case one is threatened. Unlike humans and cats, eagles mate for life and only take another partner when the first one dies. With one eye open, I watch these majestic birds soar through the air, huge wings spread wide, gracefully dipping and swirling with the pure pleasure of being.

Mom and *dad* have settled into their new life in Central Florida. They joined the Mount Dora Yacht Club where the only prerequisite is that you cannot have a yacht because no boat over thirty feet can get through the Dora Canal that separates Lake Dora from Lake Eustis where there is another short canal called *Dead River* that goes into Lake Harris. Most people here have "Woodies" or antique boats that they clean and polish themselves instead of having someone do it for them as is the norm in Miami Beach. They even know how to repair their own boats with old parts they find from places on back roads that sell Marine stuff. We purchase an eighteen-foot

1956 Chris-Craft Sea Skiff and whizz around the lake being careful to avoid the multitude of alligators that swim in pairs each spring with their heads above water. I hide in *mom's* lap when I spot them, knowing they would consider me a delicious fat treat. It is important to be courteous to the people fishing in the lakes and we remember to cut our speed when we pass small boats with lines cast for bass. Locals who have grown up on the Harris Chain of seven lakes take their boats through the Dora Canal to the famous "Gator Hole" on the northwest side of Lake Eustis where they drag large worms along the bottom of a fifteen foot deep hole that extends over two hundred feet hidden under Kissimmee grass, reeds and bulrushes. Largemouth bass that can exceed ten pounds in weight have been brought to the surface by a few lucky fishermen to offer proof that "fish tales" truly exist.

We would like to take our little boat north to the huge St. John's River which, like the Nile, flows north instead of south. We have been told it is the most spectacular sight in all of Florida. However, we're not experienced enough to manage the rough waters of Lake Monroe or navigate shallow Lake George, the second largest lake in Florida, where the center channel is only around ten feet deep and even veteran boaters get stuck on the bottom if they drift off course. When our friends invite us to join their yearly expedition to Palatka for the crab festival, we pack just enough so as not to create a burden of weight on their antique boat, also known in these parts as a "Woodie". We hop aboard, help pull up the bumpers that protect the beautiful varnished wood, push the boat with all our might away from the dock and pretend we are experienced boaters. The rules are that everyone must wear a life vest, even the cat, but it seems that life vests are only made for dogs. *Mom* bought a dog vest that would fit a Scottie Scotch Terrier to approximate my weight. While I squirm and complain, she straps it around me.

Half-way across Lake Monroe black clouds appear. The storm hits us head-on and the water suddenly becomes so rough it rocks the twenty-six foot boat without mercy. I cannot even see the lake through the windshield. I fear my dream of the Spanish Armada has come true and that we will all drown. But, Dean, our captain and owner of the prized twenty-eight foot 1939 Hutchinson, doesn't seem at all nervous as he grips the wheel to steady our course.

And then, we are out of it. We see Brackish Lake George directly ahead at the south end of the St. John's River. The sky has turned blue and cloudless. Osprey, as large as our eagles, perch on nests on top of the channel markers all the way into the St. John's River. If we continued north, we could set up camp and hunt turkeys in the 120,000 acres preserved by the river's marsh wildlife management. We are, however, only at the mouth of this awesome river where the saline-salty water is a Mecca for Blue Crab fishermen. Traps and nets are everywhere, making it necessary for us to zigzag around to protect our propellers. We carefully maneuver the boat into the narrow end of the river as it twists into a classic oxbow of pacified water where tiny boats blanket the shoreline in search of largemouth bass, speckled perch (crappie), and bluegill that inhabit this fishermen's paradise.

We cut our motor and drift into Palatka to dock the boat among hundreds of others floating beside each other and join the throng of tourists devouring spicy boiled crab, crab cakes, crab salad, dirty shrimp, and alligator tail. As soon as I taste the shrimp and crab that have been brought in directly from water to shore, I know I will never again be satisfied with those we purchase from a store. Although a favorite feast is called "Dirty

Shrimp", I find them most succulent grilled over an open fire or simply boiled with or without seasonings, and served in their shells to peel at the table.

Pâté de foie gras was fine for Queen Marie Antoinette. Elegant presentations of gourmet cuisine served under umbrellas in the surroundings of the beautiful shops in Bal Harbour and trendy Art Deco are fine for those who like happenings. But for my palette, the real food of Central Florida food outclasses them all.

Brackish Crab Chowder
Quick and easy
Yield: 8 cups

The combination of fresh ginger and bay leaf gives this chowder a lingering tangy flavor that is pungent but softer than the addition cayenne. Chopped fresh tomato, scallion greens and corn create a lovely color presentation in the white soup.

4 cups cooked blue crab meat
2 cups concentrated chicken
  or vegetable broth
  (preferably organic)
1 cup diced red onion
1 teaspoon finely minced
  ginger
1 dried or 2 fresh bay leafs
1 teaspoon salt or to taste
¼ teaspoon black pepper

3 tablespoons all-purpose
  flour mixed with ⅓ cup
  cool water
2 cups fat free half-and- half
Optional: 2 cups fresh corn
  kernels, preferably bi-color
Seeded and coarsely chopped
  plum tomatoes to top each
  serving
Chopped chives or scallion
  greens to top each serving

1. Combine the vegetable broth, onion, ginger, bay leaf, salt and pepper in a pot and bring to a boil. Reduce heat to medium. Cover and boil gently 10 minutes.
2. Combine the flour with the water and stir into the soup. Slowly stir in the half-and-half, cooking until soup has thickened. Add corn kernels, if desired.
3. Ladle into bowls and sprinkle the chopped tomatoes and chives (scallion greens) on top.
   Gluten intolerant: Exchange 1 large boiled or microwaved potato for the flour. When the potato is very soft, combine it with the broth in a blender. When thick and smooth, stir into the chowder.

Blue Crab Preparation

The live Blue Crab is a fierce opponent to the gourmet chef. These little fighters have ten legs eight of which they use to navigate sideways. The pair, or pinchers, closest to their heads is their weapon for defense from their predators and to gather food. A male blue crab (or a "jimmy") has a long, narrow, inverted Y-shaped apron that looks like the Washington Monument. An immature female blue crab (or a "sally", "she-crab") has a triangular apron that resembles a pyramid. A mature female blue crab (or a "sook") has a semicircular apron somewhat the shape of the dome of the U.S. Capitol.

Set a large cooler equipped with a drainage spout outside the house. Pour in two cups Kosher salt and fill half-way with water from the hose. Empty the bag of crabs into the salted water and watch them splash about, purging themselves of an inordinate amount of filth. Let them play approximately 10 minutes before opening the spout to allow the water to drain.

Then, pour in another 2 cups salt and fill the cooler again. Let them play another 10 minutes before emptying the cooler again.

1 dozen live blue crabs	¼ cup Zatarin® or Old Bay®
1 bottle beer	Seasoning mix or another
Water	of choice

1. Fill a lobster pot, large soup pot, or double boiler with water and bring to a boil. The lobster pot is best. The double boiler is second, and the soup pot third on my list of choices. Add the beer and seasoning.
2. With a pair of barbecue type long tongs, drop crabs into the boiling water. This is no easy maneuver. These little creatures are fierce fighters. All legs and pinchers move at once in different directions to grab onto anything within reach. Often, it's each other's pinchers, making it possible to fling two or more at once into the pot. They also resist their ultimate destiny by holding on to the side of the pot. The worst scenario is allowing one's hand to come into contact with one of these tenacious pinchers!
3. Cover the pot and return the water to a full boil. Depending upon the size, boil approximately 15 minutes, or until they turn bright orange-red. If any tone of green patches or mottled gray can be detected on the shells, they need to boil a few minutes longer. Remove crabs to the sink to drain and cool.
4. Turn the crab over to expose its breast plate, or "apron". Insert a small, sharp knife in the crack at the back of the crab. The "apron" will easily pull off. You will see a covering that can range from light gray to black and fibrous threads on both sides. These spongy gills are known as "dead man's fingers". Remove them and the yellowish "mushy" center.

(Some crab aficionados eat this reproductive structure, but I prefer to discard it) Break off and discard the small pointy legs and small pinchers. Or, you can remove the other side of the shell, exposing the meat. Remove the white meat, leaving the gills underneath to discard.

5. It will appear as though there isn't any meat in the shell, but it's tucked underneath.

Palatka Crab Cakes
Yield: 6-8 cakes

1 pound (2 cups) cooked crab meat
½ cup mayonnaise or more to bind
½ cup roughly crushed saltine crackers
½ teaspoon salt
⅛ teaspoon black pepper
⅛ teaspoon powdered ginger
⅛ teaspoon hot Hungarian paprika, or more to taste

2 teaspoons lemon juice
1 tablespoon white horseradish
Vegetable spray
Chopped cilantro leaves
Chopped chives or scallion greens
Optional: Fine noodles or angel hair pasta to accompany

1. Pick through crab for shells and cartilage and set aside.
2. Combine the mayonnaise with crushed saltines, salt, pepper, ginger, hot paprika, lemon juice, and horseradish. Carefully fold in the crab meat.
3. Wash an empty tuna or salmon can, 3-inches in diameter. Fill the can to the top and turn upside down onto a hot griddle or non-stick shallow pan that has been sprayed with vegetable oil. Release the crab cake. Do this 5 more times.

Cook the cakes over medium-high heat until very brown. Turn over carefully to brown on the other side. Or, set the griddle under the broiler rather than turning the cakes over to more easily keep their perfect shapes.
4. Sprinkle chopped cilantro over the tops. Decorate the outer edge of the plate with the chopped scallions.
5. Serve with Corn and Pepper Relish.

Corn and Pepper Relish
Yield: Approximately 2 cups

1 cup cooked parti-colored corn kernels
2 yellow bell peppers
1 red bell pepper
2 orange bell peppers
12 ounce bottled sweet and hot peppers (Mt. Olive®)

1 teaspoon crushed fennel seed
1 teaspoon powdered cumin
2 tablespoons lime juice
¼ cup chopped cilantro leaves
Salt and black pepper to taste

1. Boil corn 3 minutes only, or roast in the oven*. Cut off kernels and spoon into a bowl.
2. Save ½ of each color bell pepper and set aside. Remove core and seeds from remaining peppers and flatten. Place on a large piece of foil close to the heat under the broiler. Broil until blackened.
3. When peppers are blackened, close the foil tightly over. Leave 10 minutes or longer. Remove the peppers. The skins will peel off easily. Cut into tiny squares. Combine with corn.
4. Chop the sweet and hot peppers fine and add.

5. Add the fennel, cumin, lime juice, and cilantro. Add salt and pepper to taste. Refrigerate.
6. Cut the reserved peppers into tiny squares to decorate the side of the plate. Set a crab cake in the center of the plate and surround it with the corn and pepper relish.

Note: To roast corn in oven: Preheat oven to 325°F. Cut kernels off cob. Toss in a very small amount of corn oil. Place on a baking sheet and roast 30-40 minutes, or until lightly browned. Toss occasionally so all surfaces will cook evenly.

Dirty Shrimp

From clean waters

Yield: N/A

½ pound or more shrimp per person for a feast

Ingredients measured per pound of shrimp

1 tablespoon black pepper
½ teaspoon cayenne pepper
¼ teaspoon red pepper flakes

2 cloves garlic, peeled and
    mashed
½ pound margarine

1. Melt the margarine in a saucepan. Combine black pepper, cayenne, pepper flakes, and mashed garlic. Cook over low heat at least 5 minutes. Pour into a bowl. This may be done in the morning or a day or two in advance for the flavors to incorporate together.
2. Remove heads from the shrimp. With a small, sharp knife, make a slit through the top of the shell (the shrimp's back) and wash out the dark vein under cool, running water. Dry the shrimp with paper toweling. Toss the shrimp into the margarine mixture to coat them well.

3. Preheat oven to 200°F.
4. Remove shrimp from the margarine mixture and set them into a shallow baking dish. Bake until shells are pink and flesh has turned opaque, approximately 20-25 minutes. Do not overcook.
5. Return margarine mixture to a saucepan and heat.
6. Pour margarine mixture into individual ramekins for dipping. Pile the shrimp on a platter.

Chain of Lakes Alligator Tenders

1 pound alligator tail meat, fat and sinew removed
Olive oil or melted bacon fat
Equal parts all-purpose flour and cornmeal
Chain of Lakes Seasoning

Canola or vegetable oil in equal parts mixed with peanut or grapeseed oil to measure 2 inches deep in a large skillet.

1. Pound alligator tail with a mallet. Pierce with the tongs of a fork or tip of a sharp knife. These steps tenderize the meat.
2. Cut alligator tail into thin strips. Roll in the oil (bacon fat).
3. Mix flour with the cornmeal and seasoning in a plastic or paper bag. Toss in alligator strips and shake until coated.
4. Heat oil to 360°F. Drop strips in one at a time. Do not overcrowd the pan. Fry until strips float at the top.

Chain of Lakes Seasoning

2 tablespoons ground allspice
3 tablespoons dark brown
sugar, packed
2 tablespoons garlic salt
1 teaspoon (more or less, as
desired) Cayenne pepper

1 teaspoon ground thyme
1 tablespoon onion powder
1 teaspoon cinnamon
¼ teaspoon nutmeg
½ teaspoon chili powder

Nutsy Bass
Yield: 2 servings
Quick, easy, crunchy and delicious!

2 bass fillets, skinned and
boned
Salt to sprinkle
1 jumbo egg white
½ cup crushed almonds

⅛ teaspoon white pepper
⅛ teaspoon salt
1 tablespoon unsalted butter
1 tablespoon vegetable oil
Sliced almonds

1. Sprinkle fillets lightly with salt.
2. Beat the whites with a whisk until frothy. Dip the fillets in until very moist.
3. Place almonds in a small plastic bag and crush with a mallet or rolling pin. Add white pepper and salt. Press the nuts into the fillets lavishly.
4. Combine the butter and oil in a shallow skillet. Sauté the fillets over medium heat, covered until brown on one side. Remove cover. Turn fillets over and brown the other side, tossing in almond slices to brown, being careful not to burn the almonds.

Fried Turkey
Yield: 8-10 servings

Whole fresh turkey, no larger than 12 pounds
5 gallons peanut oil (or a mixture of canola, peanut and vegetable oils)
Creole seasoning or dry seasoning of choice
Kosher salt

Optional: garlic powder
Candy thermometer for oil
Meat thermometer for turkey
Oven mitts
Turkey fryer, equipped with a burner, pot, lifting rack and thermometer.
Optional: Fire extinguisher

1. Wash and dry the turkey. The turkey must be completely dry so the oil does not pop up and splatter the chef.
2. Do not stuff the turkey.
3. Remove the tail and extra flaps of skin.
4. Rub the inside and out with seasonings of choice, salt and garlic.
5. Heat the oil to a temperature of 350°F.
6. Insert the turkey into the oil. Fry 3-5 minutes per pound, inserting the meat thermometer several times. The turkey is done when the internal temperature of the breast reaches 170°F and the internal temperature of the thigh reaches 180°F. Turkey parts, such as the breast, wings and thighs require 4-5minutes per pound to reach their temperature points.
7. Remove the turkey from the fryer. Wrap it in aluminum foil for the juices to circulate through the meat to make it tender. Allow it to rest 30 minutes to make it easier to carve. Note: The temperature of the cooking oil should be exactly 350°F. If it drops below 340°F, it will be absorbed into the

turkey. The cooking oil should not exceed 365°F, or it can begin to smoke and catch fire. Most people bring the oil temperature to 375°F and lower it immediately to 350°F when the turkey is first inserted.

Most important: Never fry a turkey in-doors, even in a garage or under an overhang attached to the house, or on a wooden deck that could catch fire. The outdoor gas burner must sit on a level dirt or grassy area. The grease will stain concrete.

Lake George Sausage Gravy and Biscuits
Yield: 4-8 servings

Sausage Gravy

12 ounce bulk package Jimmy Dean® Regular or Sage Pork Sausage

2 tablespoons all-purpose flour

2 cups whole milk or fat-free half and half, microwaved 1 minute until warm

1. Preheat oven to 400ºF.
2. Flatten the sausage on to a baking sheet covered with foil.
3. Bake until no sign of pink when cut into.
4. Remove from the foil. Cool and crumble into bite-size pieces.
5. Pour off 2 tablespoons of fat into a skillet and discard the rest.
6. Add the flour to the fat and stir until dissolved. Over medium-low heat, stir in milk (half and half) a little at a time, cooking until thickened.
7. Stir in the sausage and cook until very hot to serve.

Biscuits

2 cups unbleached all-purpose flour
1 tablespoon plus 1 full teaspoon baking powder
1 teaspoon salt

3 tablespoons solid vegetable shortening
3 tablespoons unsalted butter
1¼ cups whole buttermilk

1. Preheat oven to 425°F.
2. Sift together the flour, baking powder, and salt into a bowl.
3. Chop the shortening and butter into the flour mixture until crumbly.
4. Slowly stir in the buttermilk until thick and creamy.
5. Remove the mixture to a floured surface and pat with your palms into a circle approximately 1 inch thick. Turn the dough over itself. Pat again. Turn the dough over itself again. Pat to 1 inch thick. Cut circles with a cookie cutter or inverted drinking glass.
6. Set the biscuits close together (touching each other for soft sides – apart for crusty sides).
7. Bake 10-12 minutes. Serve immediately with the sausage gravy poured over and around.

"I am the Cat that walks by himself, and all places are alike to me."
— <u>The Cat That Walked By Himself</u>
(<u>Just So Stories</u> by Rudyard Kipling 1902)

Teegar - Sar
Tabby Cat

W<small>HEN</small> I <small>AM NOT IN</small> the midst of a real adventure, I dream. The best place to enter into this other world is upstairs in the library. One side of the room has bookcases from floor to ceiling. Four shelves are double decked with books of all descriptions. The lower ones house *mom's* computer, the fax machine and *dad's* assorted adding machines, the electric typewriter and telephone. *Dad* hasn't learned how to use a computer yet and I doubt he ever will. He could learn if he wanted to. He's real smart. He says he hasn't the time to fool around with a machine that has a mind of its own.

The other side of the room has French doors that open to a large porch overlooking the swimming pool and woods. Because it faces east, the morning sun streams through the glass panes, illuminating one section of the carpet with its warm rays. It's here that I settle myself, first stretching front and back legs while resting on my stomach. Then, as the warmth bathes my body, I turn to my side before finally rolling onto my back so my pink oval tummy can receive the full benefit of these beams of radiance. I know I look a bit silly with my little legs projecting straight up and my fluffy feet bent in a ninety degree angle parallel to the floor but I do not care.

I appear to be asleep because my eyes are tightly shut. My wispy soft lashes rest against my cheeks and my wiry nylon whiskers, four on each side, jut out from the bulges at the sides of my pink nose. As Mother Nature envelops me with her generosity, I dream sweet cat dreams.

One morning, while in the midst of my reverie, I became aware of a near-by presence. I opened one eye and looked down to the woods below. There was the largest cat I had ever seen. It must have weighed thirty pounds. Its short fur was mottled with dark brown, light brown and golden patches arranged so deliberately that the animal might have been a miniature of the tiger family. I turned over and walked downstairs to the sun room. Someone had left the door ajar and, although I knew I was not allowed to go outside, I pushed the door with my paw until the open crack had enough space for me to sneak through.

Good morning, I said. *Where did you come from and what are you doing here?*

My house is around the bend. I came to see if the new neighbors would give me a hand- out.

If you have a home, why do you want a hand out?

I said it was my house. I did not say it was my home. I like to wander. Sometimes I go a mile away into Mount Dora. There are restaurants everywhere, and a hotel and lots of bed and breakfast places. Every place has a bowl of food for the town cats. The Lakeside Inn Historic Hotel has dried kibbles on its back doorstep. Dishes of food line the sidewalks in front of almost every restaurant. The Windsor Rose Tearoom even named their favorite cat, 'Tetley'. When the restaurants forget to put out food, the town cats know they can get a hand-out at the houses on Lake Dora Road. If you ever go to town, just ask any cat how to find "Boat House Row". The houses were once boat houses jutting out from the shore on Lake Dora. Then, people began to enclose them and move in to be with their boats. Lately it has become the fashionable place to live. People regard this badly paved road filled with potholes with its hodgepodge of bad architecture as a sort of Nantucket south or Key West north. Prices have soared sky high and the old timers are selling to city folk who think of the area as chic. Remember to beg at their front doors only because there might be an alligator waiting to devour an unsuspecting cat in the back near the water.

Oh, my! I do not think I would venture near that place. How long do you stay in town?

Sometimes just a few hours, other times several days. When I become bored, I go back to my house in the country. They're always glad to see me.

I looked up into his broad forehead and enormous yellow eyes set above his pudgy cheeks and then down to his wide feet.

My name is Sakie. I am named after the delicious warm drink in Japan. If I may ask, what type feline are you?

My name is 'Teegar'. I suppose they call me that because I look like a little tiger. At the moment I can be accurately classified as a 'Domestic Shorthair',

263

*or combined Shorthairs, known as the American
Tabby Cat. But I was once the elite American
Shorthair known as the Silver Classic Tabby Cat,
whose origin goes all the way back to the European
wildcat and the early Egyptian cat. In the early
tenth century, the Romans brought my breed into
the British Isles where we protected the wheat
fields from rodents. History relates that one or even
several of my ancestors were brought over on the
Mayflower, making me eligible to become a member
of the elite society of SAR.*

SAR? Don't you mean DAR?

*The DAR is a Daughter of the American
Revolution. The SAR is a Son of the American
Revolution. Although I would not have to prove my
lineal bloodline, I would have to prove that one or
more of my ancestors aided in achieving American
independence during the Revolutionary War period
between the years, 1775-1784.*

I remember my other lives. Do you remember yours?

He stretched out on the deck in the warm rays of the sun
that shimmered across the blue water of the swimming pool.

*Let me tell you about my life as a Rebel in the
Revolutionary War. First of all, it's important
to know the terminology. The words 'Rebel' and
'Whig' referred to those colonists who supported the
Revolution and advocated total independence from*

England and its cruel, psychotic king, George III. The terms 'Loyalist' and 'Tory' were those American colonists who supported King George.

In 1848, sixty-four years after the war, American poet and author, Elizabeth Ellet, wrote a book titled Women of the American Revolution. In it she told of a brave young woman named Emily Geiger, who carried a message through dangerous British Tory territory to General Sumter to tell him to join General Greene to win the battle against the renowned Irish military genius of the British army, Lord Rawdon, also known as the Earl of Moira, and Commander Colonel Alexander Stewart from England. There were some skeptics a hundred years later who claimed her brave ride was folklore and that there was no proof in any historic record that a person named Emily Geiger even existed. I know she existed, and I know she carried out the dangerous mission. I was there.

"I know not what course others may take; but as for me, give me liberty or give me death!"
— Patrick Henry, 1775

Emily Geiger's Sar Tabby

It is a warm, breezy day in Newberry County, South Carolina in June, 1781. Emily is sitting in the parlour doing needlework and I am playing with a ball of yarn that has slipped out of her sewing box. Everyone these days is talking about the war. General Greene is camped just two miles away from our luxurious farm with his troops, who are terribly depressed after retreating from their unsuccessful assault in May on Lord Rawdon's army at Fort Ninety-six by the Saluda River. We cannot help but listen to Emily's papa talking with his neighbor about the defeat. He is recounting how Lord Rawdon's army pursued General Greene all the way across the Enoree River but did not attack General Green's cavalry which was under the command of Colonels Lee and Washington.

"Lord Rawdon is going to abandon the Fort at ninety-six."

"Is this a rumor or is it true"

"It's true. General Greene received the intelligence this morning. Rawdon will move his regiment from Charleston to Friday's Perry on the Congaree where he will join Col. Stuart. Their forces will be divided. Greene proposes to follow Rawdon and attack."

Emily's father was confused. "Why did he not fight him at the Saluda?"

"Because General Sumter was not there, and now he will not be able to join him because no one is willing to bring the message to him. The entire area is filled with Tories who are elated by our defeat at Ninety-Six. They are a dangerous group who will murder any man who brings a message to Sumter."

Tears came to Emily's father. "Oh, that I were able", said the old man. "If I were not an invalid, I would set forth this very night."

Emily set her needlework down. "What do you think, Tabby? Can we do it?" I looked up at her, and tried to convey my thoughts that she was an eighteen year-old female in a male world involved in the worst war in history. She misinterpreted my stance and said, "I can see that you are a brave cat dedicated to the same cause as I. We will do this deed together."

The next morning we went to General Greene's camp.

"I will be our messenger", she said.

"But, you are a girl."

"I am a Patriot."

He took out his quill and dipped it into the ink pot on his desk. As he wrote the letter to General Sumter, he verbally communicated the contents to Emily in the event it was lost. Then he summoned his finest horse to be brought to him. Emily attached a pouch to her waist and settled me safely within. A mounting block was set by the left side of the animal. Emily swung her right leg around the fixed head and found the stirrup with her left foot, mounting in side position the broadest part of the saddle set square to the horse's back with her seat perfectly balanced. He began to trot and then quickened his pace into the three-beat gait of a canter.

We had a feeling we were being followed. It had to be a Tory tipped off by one of General Green's neighbors. One never knew whom to trust any more. Even good people would give us away if they were on the side of the British. We rode faster for many hours until we were so exhausted we could go no farther. Finally, Emily said,

"Tabby, I cannot ride on. A friend of my father's lives in this area. He's a Tory, but I think he can be trusted to protect us."

We pulled the horse to a stop and dismounted. The door was immediately opened by an elderly gentleman and his kindly faced wife.

"Good gracious, my child! What are you doing so far from home? These are dangerous times. You do not know who might be lurking in the dark. We were about to have our supper. I will set another place."

I began to salivate from the aroma of an Apple Pan Dowdy bubbling in an igloo shaped brick oven that seemed to be attached to the side of the fireplace. She helped Emily off with her cape and removed me from the pouch while her husband went outside to give our horse water and food. When he returned, she set down a saucer of milk for me with the delicious head of the four pound whole rainbow trout she had cooked. The table was also filled with steamed lobsters from the Atlantic Ocean. Lobster in Colonial times was so abundant that it was used by the Native Americans to fertilize their fields. It

*was considered poverty food that was fed to children
and prisoners. No one in those days would have
believed it would become an expensive delicacy.
She also gave me a slice of their shrimp and corn
pie. While I separated the shrimp from the corn,
they inquired about the health of Emily's father but
asked no questions about her strange appearance and
journey. After dinner they sent us directly to bed.*

*We slept only a short time when the sound of hoofs
approaching the house awakened us. Emily sat
straight up and listened. Downstairs she heard a man
introduce himself as Billy Mink, a Tory. He was
asking our hosts if they had seen us. She put her finger
to her lips to silence any purr I might have made
and tiptoed across the room where she quickly dressed.
Grabbing her possessions and fastening the pouch
around her waist, she pushed me in and crawled out
the window. As she saddled our horse she said,*

"Keep watch, Tabby. If you see anything, purr softly."

*She reached up and, grabbing the saddle with her
right hand, shinnied up the side of the horse with
her left leg and jumped onto the saddle without a
groom's help or a mounting block. The horse moved
at a canter across the muddy farmland that had just
been plowed instead of the hard ground where our
horse could have been detected. The second its hoofs
touched the tall grass, she forced the stallion into a
roaring gallop, pressing her right calf against the
saddle and her left thigh into the leaping head to lock*

into an 'emergency grip' that would keep her locked into the saddle during a ride that would take us over uneven ground and fallen trees.

We rode all night until dawn before we stopped at a home she knew to be occupied by Whigs. The man removed the saddle, rubbed down the perspiration dripping from the exhausted horse, and wiped the white foam from its mouth. Then, he placed the saddle on his fastest stallion.

"Your horse has been pushed awfully hard. Take it a bit easier with this one."

"It wasn't always me who forced him on. Each time he began to slow his pace, Tabby reached his claws out of the pouch and dug them into the poor beast's flesh."

"You are a fine American," *he said, and scratched the happy spot at the top of my head.*

An hour later, after we had feasted on South Carolina breakfast of baked eggs with sausage and shrimp over hominy, we set off again with a bag filled with sugared pecans to nibble on during the ride.

Our new horse was fast and powerful with much greater stamina than the previous one, but as the sun turned into a huge orange ball and began to descend over the earth's western perimeter, three men came out of the woods, blocking our path and causing us to make an abrupt stop. They were wearing the red coats and cocked three cornered hats of the British battalion.

"We are taking you to the headquarters of Lord Rawdon. Do not attempt to get away, or we will have to shoot you", *said the man in the middle. He lifted a heavy musket used in battle and pointed it directly at us. The two men on either side held light field guns at their sides in anticipation of our possible but not probable escape. I began to shake uncontrollably. Emily placed her hand on my head and answered in a strong voice without flinching,*

"I have nothing to hide. I will gladly accompany you."

When we reached the headquarters we were immediately taken to Lord Rawdon. He also was dressed in a red coat. He did not look like a dangerous warrior, but rather like an English gentleman. We knew differently. If he found the letter to General Greene, he would murder us both without conscience. We could detect the aromas of Oxtail Stew boiling in a huge cast iron pot for the soldiers and expensive Venison and Prime Rib of Beef with Yorkshire Pudding simmering on the hearth for the noblemen, but we were offered none.

"Lock her up in the back room until Mrs. Hogabook arrives to search her."

The officers took Emily by the arm and escorted her to the room, where they promptly closed and locked the door behind us.

"Tabby, what shall we do with the letter? If I tear it up, they will find the pieces and, if I don't, they will know General Greene's plans. I have already memorized its contents so I do not really need it."

I grabbed the paper from her hand and, securing it with my paw, tore it into several pieces with my teeth. Then I began to eat the pieces, swallowing them as quickly as possible. She began to grab at the pieces also and shoved them, one by one, into her mouth to do the same. Before we could get rid of all the evidence, we heard someone coming. It was Mrs. Hogabook. Emily grabbed a handful of papers and pushed them into her mouth. When the woman opened the door, Emily turned her back and cupped her hands over her face while making a huge sobbing noise while she gulped down the papers.

Mrs. Hogabook immediately searched Emily's clothing and my pouch. After she stole our delicious pecan snacks, she told her to remove her clothing so she could search her body. As she lifted her skirt, the last piece of paper fell to the floor. I quickly covered it with my paw, stretched out with my face in the opposite direction and popped it into my mouth. I had just swallowed the last bit when Mrs. Hogabook said, "Now, pick up your cat so I can search him." Emily grabbed me around my stomach, and letting my feet dangle, held me up for her to examine. A few minutes later, after looking carefully around the room for hiding places and finding nothing, she left.*

Lord Rawdon was extremely embarrassed and apologized profusely to us for the inconvenience. Unaware that the 'friend' she claimed she was going to visit was a Whig, he arranged for an escort to take us to her 'friend's' home.

273

When we arrived, the escort galloped back to Lord Rawdon's camp. As soon as he was out of sight, we were saddled up with a fresh horse and informed of a shortcut to our destination.

We rode through the woods for several hours until we reached a clearing where we could see patriots dressed in blue uniforms. The soldiers saw us also and raised their weapons. When they realized the rider was a young girl with a cat, they put down their guns and greeted us warmly. Then they escorted us to the camp.

A very tall soldier lifted Emily out of the saddle, holding her skirts close to her body so as not to expose her legs. When he set her on her feet, she exclaimed breathlessly,

"I have a message from General Greene for General Sumter."

The soldiers were so amazed at this statement they asked no questions, but immediately escorted us to the General's quarters.

General Sumter was elated to see us. He kissed Emily on both cheeks and scratched the top of my head.

"Please sit down and tell me your mission"

Emily sat and 'read' the entire letter from memory, word for word.

"So, if General Greene and I combine forces, we can attack the isolated British posts established to protect the Loyalist population, capture them and break them up. If we can destroy Stewart's forces, we could end the British threat to the south once and for all and prepare for a siege at Yorktown."

And, that is exactly what happened. The very tall soldier escorted Emily and me safely home to her proud father where his friends proclaimed her the heroine of the Revolutionary war.

Is that all, I asked?

Not quite. When the war was over, the tall soldier came back and asked Emily for her hand in marriage. He also brought his cat, a beautiful silver Tabby that looked like me except smaller. We all lived together happily ever after in independence from the wicked King of England.

Tell me another story, I begged.

I'll be off now.

He stretched his huge body, stood up, and strode stealthily around the lounge chairs on the pool deck, making his way into the woods towards the back gate.

In my younger days I could have fallen in love with this brave, yet gentle Tabby whose lineage went all the way back to the Mayflower.

I was about to chortle, *you are a fine American and truly qualify for top membership in the SAR,* but he had disappeared.

Emily's Breakfast Feast
Shrimp with Hominy
Yield: Approximately 4 servings, 5 shrimp per serving

Traditionally, the hominy for grits was ground by a stone mill. Grits are commonly made of alkali-treated corn known as hominy.

The Shrimp

20 large raw fresh shrimp (21-25 or 26-30 per pound), peeled with tails on
¼ cup olive oil
¼ cup fresh lime juice (about 2 limes)
½ cup orange juice
¼ cup cilantro, chopped
2 cloves garlic, minced, or 1 teaspoon garlic powder
1 large shallot, minced, or ½ teaspoon onion powder
1 teaspoon coriander
2 tablespoons Worcestershire sauce
½ teaspoon kosher salt
⅛ teaspoon cayenne pepper or more to taste
¼ tsp freshly ground black pepper

1. Peel and devein the shrimp, leaving the shells on their tails for presentation. Set aside.
2. Combine remaining ingredients and toss with the shrimp. Cover and refrigerate 1 hour only.
3. Remove the shrimp from the marinade. Pour the marinade into a saucepan.
4. Set the shrimp on a hot, non-stick griddle and quickly sear on both sides until just done. Do not overcook.
5. Bring the marinade to a boil, stirring. Cook 1 minute. Remove from the heat. Toss in the shrimp.

6. Set a good helping of Cheese Grits in the center of a wide rim soup bowl or plate and place the shrimp with the marinade around the edge.

Hominy (Cheese Grits)
Yield: 4 cups

2 ½ cups chicken broth
4 cups fat free half & half
1 cup (8 ounces) hominy
white grits (not instant)
4 tablespoons butter
½ teaspoon salt (to Taste)

½ teaspoon white pepper
½ cup (4 ounces) Gruyere or
Gouda or mixed Mexican
cheese, chopped fine
½ cup grated Parmesan
cheese

1. Bring the broth and half and half to a boil. Add the butter.
2. Stir in the grits and return to a boil.
3. Stir in the butter, salt and white pepper.
4. Reduce heat to low.
5. Cover the pot and cook 20-25 minutes or until soft and creamy, stirring from the bottom several times so mixture does not stick.
6. Remove from the heat. Stir in the cheeses. Cover. Let the mixture sit 10 minutes, or until the cheese has melted into the grits. Stir. Serve.
   Note: The grits can be made in advance and transferred to a casserole dish. Cover and place in a preheated 200°F oven.

Egg and Sausage Casserole
The Whig's breakfast
Yield: 6-8 servings

3-4 slices Italian or white bread with crusts
1 pound bulk pork or turkey sausage
1½ cups chopped American or sharp English Cheddar cheese, or mixed cheeses of choice
6 jumbo graded eggs
½ teaspoon salt
Optional: Pinch of white pepper or cayenne or hot Hungarian paprika

1 ½ cup whole milk
Optional: 1 small onion, chopped fine
Optional: ½ cup chopped green chilies or seasoned diced tomatoes.
5X9X3 or 10X7X3 baking dish or other casserole
¾ cup additional chopped cheese

1. The night before: Grease the bottom and sides of the dish with butter or oil or spray with vegetable spray. This is not necessary when using an aluminum disposable pan. Slice the bread and cover the bottom.
2. Slice or flatten the sausage. Brown in a shallow skillet or cook in the oven until done. Pour off the fat. Crumble the sausage and cover the bread.
3. Sprinkle the cheese over the sausage. (Cover with the onion /chilies/tomatoes).
4. Beat the eggs with salt and pepper. Sprinkle with a pinch of white pepper or cayenne. Add milk, beating smooth. Pour over the cheese. Cover with foil. Refrigerate overnight.
5. Preheat oven to 350°F.

6. Bake, covered, approximately 50 minutes. Remove foil. Sprinkle the top with the reserved cheese and continue baking until melted and bubbly. Serve with your choice of hot or mild tomato salsa on the side.

South Carolina Shrimp and Corn Pie
Yield: 6 servings

1 cup cooked and cleaned small shrimp

2 cups cooked corn or 15 ounce can

2 jumbo graded eggs, beaten slightly

½ cup warm whole milk or fat free half and half

1 teaspoon Worcestershire sauce

¼ teaspoon mace

⅛ teaspoon white pepper

2 tablespoons melted unsalted butter

Salt to taste

8X8 casserole dish, buttered

1. Preheat oven to 325°F
2. Cook and clean shrimp. Scrape corn kernels from cobs.
3. Beat eggs slightly. Combine with the shrimp and corn. Stir in the milk, Worcestershire, mace, white pepper and melted butter. Stir in salt to taste.
4. Butter the casserole dish, and pour in the filling.
5. Bake 30 minutes. When an inserted knife comes out clean, the pie is done.

This delicate freshwater fish stands on its own merit without embellishment of herbs and spices. Serve with fresh green asparagus tossed with chopped tarragon or cilantro leaves and garlic mashed potatoes.

Freshwater Trout with Georgia Pecans
Yield: 2 servings
If the trout are large, 1 can serve 2 persons

2 freshwater trout, cleaned
and skinned
Salt to sprinkle
Juice of ½ lemon
1 jumbo egg white, beaten to
the frothy stage

⅓ cup or more ground pecans
to cover
1 tablespoon unsalted butter
1 tablespoon extra-virgin
olive oil

1. Wash the trout under cold water and dry on paper toweling. Separate the two sides by cutting with a sharp knife.
2. If the skin has not been removed, carefully insert the point of a very sharp knife under the narrow end of the fish and gently pull off the skin by holding the fish down with one hand while removing the skin with the other. If the fish is fresh, this will be achieved easily. If it has been frozen, it will be more difficult.
3. Squeeze lemon juice over both sides and sprinkle lightly with sea salt
4. Beat an egg white to the frothy stage and dip the fillets in to cover.
5. Cover heavily with the pecans, patting them into the fish on both sides.
6. Heat the butter and olive oil to medium in a heavy bottom skillet.
7. Sauté the fish on both sides until golden brown. Do not overcook.
   Note: Watch the pecan crust that it does not burn. Check the heat of your stove.

Steamed Lobster
Yield: N/A
Whole lobsters
Pot of boiling water

1. Bring the water to a boil. Drop live lobsters in head first. Bring the water back to a full boil. Cover the pot with the top tilted for steam to escape and so the water will not boil over the sides.
2. Boil 12-13 minutes for 1 pound lobster, 15 minutes for 1 ½ pounds, 20 minutes for 1 ¾ - 2 pounds. When lobsters are red without any trace of black mottling, they are cooked.
3. Remove from the water. Split the back shell from the head to the tail. Remove and discard the spongy sack between the eyes. Pull out the black vein that runs along the tail.
4. Serve with melted butter.

Bourbon Pecans
For the ride

Yield: 2 pounds

2 pounds Georgia pecan halves
2 cups granulated sugar
¼ cup Kentucky bourbon
1 cup bottled water
¼ cup light Karo® syrup
1 tablespoon cinnamon
⅛ teaspoon nutmeg
2 cups granulated sugar

1. Preheat oven to 250°F.
2. Empty the pecans into a large bowl.
3. Combine 2 cups granulated sugar with the bourbon, water, syrup, cinnamon, and nutmeg in a saucepan. Bring to a boil

over high heat. Boil 2 minutes. Reduce heat to medium and boil another 3 minutes. Pour over the pecans, a little at a time, tossing well after each addition, until the nuts are well coated.

4. Toss with 2 cups granulated sugar.
5. Remove to 2 large baking sheets that have been covered with a double layer parchment paper. Try to keep the nuts separated.
6. Set the baking sheets into the oven. Reduce oven temperature to 200°F.
7. Bake 35 minutes. With a spatula, turn the nuts over. Bake another 35 minutes.
8. Flip the nuts from the top piece of parchment to the one underneath for them to finish baking on a dry sheet. Turn off the oven. Return the nuts to the oven to crisp.
9. Store in airtight containers.

Apple Pan Dowdy
Yield: Approximately 8 servings
Deep dish, preferably Pyrex® or ovenproof
glass baking dish, 8 ½ X5 ½ X 3 inches

For the Apples:

6 large Granny Smith or Rome apples, peeled and sliced*

1 tablespoon lemon juice

½ cup dark brown sugar

¼ teaspoon nutmeg

1 teaspoon cinnamon

½ cup dark Karo® syrup or maple syrup

½ cup water

4 tablespoons butter

1. Preheat oven to 425°F.

2. Peel and slice the apples lengthwise ½ inch thick. Toss with the lemon juice and set into a baking dish, preferably oven-proof glass.
3. Mix the sugar, nutmeg, and cinnamon together in a micro-waveable bowl. Add the syrup and water. Cut up the butter and add. Cover and microwave 25 seconds.
4. Pour over the apples and toss to combine.
   *For a less tart preparation, the Fiji apple can be substituted.

For the topping:

1 cup all-purpose flour	4 tablespoons butter or lard
½ teaspoon salt	(Lard was used originally
1 full tablespoon baking	in this recipe for a flaky
powder	topping)
¼ cup granulated sugar	½ cup whole milk

1. Combine the flour, salt, baking powder, and sugar. Cut the butter (lard) into it until it resembles small pebbles.
2. Fold in the milk.
3. Drop by spoonsful over the apple mixture.
4. Bake 10 minutes. Reduce heat to 350°F and bake 35 minutes longer.
5. Serve warm with ice cream of choice.

Oxtail Stew for the British Army
Yield: 4 servings

Oxtail Stew or "Ragû" became a British staple for the working class. It might have been brought to the British Isles from France in the 17ᵗʰ century by the persecuted Huguenots who fled when Louis X1V revoked the Edict of Nantes. Many a stockpot throughout Europe was made tastier by the Huguenots, who were known for their culinary expertise.

3-4 pounds beef oxtails cut 2 inches thick
Salt and pepper
Flour to dredge
¼ cup chopped porcini dried mushrooms
1 cup vegetable oil (to cover the bottom of a large skillet)
1-2 cloves garlic, minced
1 green bell pepper, chopped
1 large onion, chopped
1 tablespoon minced fresh parsley
1 teaspoon minced fresh thyme, or 2 teaspoons dried
1 teaspoon minced fresh oregano, or 2 teaspoons powdered

A sprig of rosemary, or 2 teaspoons dried
Several fresh basil leaves or 1 teaspoon dried
1 bay leaf
1 cup cabernet sauvignon red wine
1 ¼ cups rich beef broth (10 ounce can)
3 tablespoons tomato paste
14.5 ounce canned, diced tomatoes with Italian or Mexican herbs
8 or more red bliss potatoes
Baby carrots, or large carrots, sliced thick

1. Preheat oven to 350°F.
2. Rinse the porcini mushrooms with warm water. Soak in hot water to soften. Pour off the water. Rinse again. Chop fine.
3. Season the oxtails with salt and pepper. Put flour in a bag and shake a few at a time to coat.
4. Cover the bottom of a large skillet with vegetable oil and place over high heat. Brown the oxtails on both sides and remove from the skillet.
5. Combine mushrooms, garlic, green pepper, onion, parsley, thyme, oregano, rosemary, basil, bay leaf, wine, beef broth, tomato paste and diced tomatoes in a deep roaster and toss with the oxtail pieces. Cover the roaster tightly and set into the oven. Roast 3½ hours or until very tender. Cool completely. Refrigerate several hours or overnight.
6. Remove the fat that has congealed at the top of the gravy. Cover the roaster and reheat in a 300°F oven for 35-40 minutes, or until very hot.
7. Cover carrots with water and boil until tender. Cut a small strip around each potato so the skins will not pop open. Cover with water and boil, covered, until tender.
8. Spoon oxtails and gravy into a large serving bowl and cover with the carrots and potatoes. Serve with fresh bread or rolls to mop up the gravy.

British Landowner's
Grilled Venison Filets
Yield: 4 servings

Beef filets can be substituted

2 large portobello mushrooms	4 venison filets, cut 1 inch
6 tablespoons unsalted butter	thick from the tenderloin
1 clove fresh garlic	4 slices French bread, toasted
Salt	on one side only
Coarse black pepper	

1. Clean mushrooms but do not soak in water. Remove stems. Slice. Melt 4 tablespoons of the butter in a skillet. Peel and crush (or chop) garlic and cook over the lowest heat for 1 minute. Carefully add mushrooms and cook quickly over medium-high heat two minutes only. (Turn with a spatula so they will not break into pieces) Remove pan from heat. Do not overcook.

2. Sprinkle filets lightly with salt and pepper. Melt two table-spoons butter and brush the steaks on one side. Place on a hot grill or under the broiler on the top rack and brown. Turn, brush again, and brown on the other side. Re-heat the mushrooms over a medium fire.

3. Place a slice of French bread on each plate, toast side down. Set a filet on top of each and spoon the mushrooms and sauce from the pan over. Serve immediately.

   Note: Check desired temperature with a meat thermometer (Rare: 120-125°F, Medium: 130-135°F, Well done: 140-145°F), or press the tops with a fork. If very spongy, meat is rare. The firmer the meat to the touch, the more done it is within. If too rare for your taste, remove the filets to the mushroom pan and cook for a minute over medium heat. Do not overcook.

Jolly Old England's Prime Rib Roast
Approximately 8-10 servings

It is difficult to estimate the exact size of the beef to serve because of the weight of the bones. It is better to have left-overs than not enough. A quick guesstimate would be:
3-rib roast = 6 people
4-rib roast = 8 people
5-rib roast = 10 people

First 5 ribs roast of beef, bone in
Freshly ground black pepper
Optional: Dry steak seasoning to rub
Optional: 1-2 cloves garlic
Kosher or coarse sea salt

2 tablespoons melted butter or olive oil
3 Bermuda onions, sliced thick
2 ribs celery sliced thin
1 ¼ cup beef broth (10 ounce can)

1. Several hours before roasting, trim off as much fat as possible without cutting into the meat. Sprinkle the beef and bones with salt and black pepper. Optional: For extra flavor, rub the meat with dry steak seasoning. If you like garlic, rub a clove or two over the beef. Discard the clove.
2. Preheat oven to 450°F.
3. Bring the beef to room temperature. Sprinkle with salt. Brush or rub with butter (oil). Line a roasting pan with the

onions and celery and place the beef on top, fat side up. Pour the broth into the bottom of the pan.

4. Roast, uncovered, 15 minutes. Reduce temperature to 325°F and cook until done to your liking. Turn the beef over the last 20 minutes to brown the bones.

5. To slice: Cut the bones off before slicing. Serve with gravy and white horseradish on the side.

6. Cooking time: If you have a meat thermometer, remove the roast from the oven when it registers 125°F. - rare beef, 130°F- medium-rare, 140°F. - medium, and 150°F. -well-done. Let the meat stand 15-20 minutes before carving. The juices will settle and the texture will be firmer, allowing easier carving. It will continue to cook internally as it stands. If you do not have a thermometer, follow the method below. Cooking time includes the first twenty minutes. Do not baste at any time. Regardless of the weight of the beef, it should not take longer than 2 ½ hours to cook through

Rare	15-18 minutes per pound
Medium-rare	18-20 minutes per pound
Medium	22-24 minutes per pound
Well-done	26-30 minutes per pound

Yorkshire Pudding
Yield: approximately 4 servings

3 jumbo eggs, beaten
1½ cups fat-free half and half
1½ cups all-purpose sifted
  flour
½ heaping teaspoon baking
  powder

¼ teaspoon salt
⅛ teaspoon white pepper
4 tablespoons butter or
  drippings from the beef to
  cover the bottom of the pan
9X9 inch pan

1. Beat the eggs with a wire whisk or hand-held electric mixer.
2. Add the half & half, beating until smooth.
3. Add the flour all at once and beat until smooth.
4. Cover the bowl and refrigerate several hours or until very cold.
5. Preheat oven to 450°F.
6. Remove from the refrigerator and let the batter stand at room temperature 15 minutes before beating again until smooth.
7. Set the pan with the butter (drippings) in the oven. When the butter has melted and the pan is hot, pour in the batter.
8. Bake 10 minutes.
9. Reduce oven temperature to 400°F.
10. Bake 15 minutes longer.
11. Reduce oven temperature to 350°F.
12. Bake approximately 10 more minutes or until puffed and brown on top.
13. Cut into squares and serve immediately with gravy or butter on the side.

"Cats are smarter than dogs. You can't get eight cats to pull a sled through snow."
— Jeff Valdez

Sam Sends Freeway

I WAS THE FIRST TO SEE it. I was sleeping on the window ledge in the sunroom. The past two days had been the coldest of the year, with the temperature dropping below thirty degrees, a potential disaster for the citrus of Central Florida. Basking in the warmth of the morning sun with one eye open, I saw a furry shadow moving around the back woods. It was obviously a member of the canine family, and it looked to be about eight months old. It moved toward the house and then stopped at the swimming pool where it put its whole head in and slurped up enough water to fill the pool again. I could see that it was a he-dog. He looked as though he had not had food or drink for days. He was about twelve inches tall with a body that was a bit longish, legs that were a bit shortish, and a tail definitely too long for both. His blond fur was dirty and matted. Hair covered his whole face including the eyes, but his tail was just a long bone that protruded in an arc from behind. He was the scruffiest mutt I had ever seen.

Dad saw him also. He dropped what he was doing and ran outside. When the strange animal saw him, he ran into the woods. *Dad* called to *mom* to bring some leftover chicken from dinner. Setting it by the pool, she sneaked behind the cabaña door so as not to be seen. He moved cautiously toward the food, looking around suspiciously. Then he plopped his whole face into the dish and inhaled the chicken in one gulp. *Mom* walked slowly from behind the door. He saw her and immediately scurried back into the woods. This performance repeated itself for the next two days.

The third day when *mom* brought food outside, she sat on the steps at the back door instead of hiding in the cabaña. He moved stealthily from the woods and devoured the mound of chicken, which had now been mixed with dog food purchased from the supermarket. Instead of dashing back into the woods, he turned and raced in *mom's* direction with such fervor it appeared she was about to be attacked. With one leap the stupid canine toppled her onto her back. Then he jumped on her chest and slurped her face and ears and hair with all his might. From my vantage point I could read a sign that hung around his neck, invisible to her but clear as day to me. On it was written, *Sam Sent Me.* This had to be some sort of cruel joke. Sam would never send something that looked or acted like this. He had too much class. I knew immediately that this scruffy interloper was about to present a major problem to an eleven year-old pampered feline of royal ancestry.

They went to all the houses in the vicinity to find his family. Some of the neighbors had seen him making his way down the highway. One neighbor saw him race away when the neighbor next to him took a broom and whacked him off his front porch. Finally, about a quarter mile away, a lady said she knew where he came from. She was watering the plants by her front porch when she noticed a truck driving much slower than the speed limit. She said that it came to a stop and the front door was quickly thrown open and then immediately closed. Then, the truck gathered up speed so fast it covered the road with a trail of dust. The next thing she saw was a dog standing in the road. She walked up to him and saw he was wearing a collar. She removed it and went into her house to try to find a name or number to call from the tag. When she came outside again, the dog was gone. She handed the collar to *dad.*

Dad tracked down the owner through the rabies ID written on the tag. A man answered on the first ring.

"Excuse me", said *dad*, "but did you lose a dog on the highway outside Mount Dora?"

"Why," asked the man?

"Because I think we found him."

"If I'd wanted that dog, I would have found him myself. Don't call this number again!"

There was a click. He had hung up.

They took him to my new Mount Dora veterinarian, who checked him out and then punctured him a dozen times with anti-everything to cure him from any diseases he might have and all that he might be exposed to. Then they brought him home and scrubbed him with *mom's* best shampoo.

He was ready to bring into the house.

He raced inside all happy and stupid. Then he saw me in the distance sleeping in the overstuffed leather chair in front of the television set in our family room.

A squirrel, he barked happily. *No, I think it's a rabbit,* he yelped as he moved closer. *Wow. It's a Cat! Kill the Cat! Kill the Cat!*

You Truck Trash, I hissed, *don't you know who I am? I rule this house. I am a Princess and you had better mind your manners, if you have any.*

I raised my paw up to warn him he was about to get his nose scratched bloody. He was so dumb he didn't even know I was clawless. He backed off for the moment. The drama was about to begin.

"Yesterday I was a dog. Today I am a dog. Tomorrow I will probably still be a dog. Sigh. There's so little hope for advancement."
— Snoopy, from <u>Peanuts,</u> by Charles Schultz

Freeway Takes Over

THEY NAMED HIM FREEWAY, WHICH was logical because that's where he came from. It was also the name of the dog in the old television series, "Hart to Hart" that my family watched faithfully through the years. My vet scribed him into the records as "A Benji Mix". I couldn't have written a better insult if I tried. Benji, from the movie by the same title, was a multiple mixture of pedigrees, known as a mongrel or mutt. Webster's Dictionary defines the word "mutt" as the shortened version of "muttonhead", "a stupid or insignificant person - a fool". This four-legged creature that had gained admittance into my domain exceeded any definition.

Within a few months hair began to grow on his tail. It grew and grew and grew into a thick, long silky mane with straight hairs separated from each other in blond luxuriance. I was the first to notice that the tail curled upward touching his back. The hair fanned out like one of those pom-poms waved by cheerleaders at a football game. It had become the plume of a pedigree Spitz or Pomeranian. And that was where the resemblance ended. The tail was in such contrast to the thick curled fur growing on his body and legs I was sure I was looking at two different dogs. His legs were too short for his stocky body that was too long. The hair that covered his round head also covered his big round dark brown eyes, and his ears hung past his chin covered by the same long, blond silky hair as his tail. Within these hairs, however, were a few strands of black that sometimes appeared prominent and at other times disappeared. One of our friends was sure he was a Tibetan terrier, perhaps even a cousin of the purebred champion at Westminster Kennel Club. Right! In his dreams!

My final assessment was that, if he ever lived another life, it was as a centipede. He had a habit of speed-walking the long driveway instead of running. His four short little legs moved in unison so fast they looked exactly like a ten-legged arthropod with jointed appendages. When he broke into a run in the field and through the grove, it seemed as though he was trying to outrun the wind that sent his fur flying in such a manner he appeared to be taking off the ground. With his long mane of a tail pointed straight up and the hair rustling like a giant flag behind him, he could cover fifteen acres in the time it took to call his name.

His appearance was totally different when he was being bathed. The water flattened his fluffy exterior, exposing his true shape. His head wasn't wide at all but an angular shape like a Cocker Spaniel's, and what we all thought was a square burly jaw was actually an elongated weak looking snout camouflaged by long furry whiskers. The strong body that appeared stocky under his massive coat was actually quite thin. The little short legs were nothing but bony strips. He was a phony, a scrawny kid with football padding that made him appear a tough Jocko. But lest I fool myself, the kid was straight from the back alleys of a tough upbringing not to be messed with.

He loved everyone and everything and everyone loved him. Everyone that is, except me. He came at me the second day. Before anyone realized what was happening, he chased me into a corner and then leaped spread-eagle over my back. I could hear the 'splat' of him colliding with my prosperous obesity. Then he stood and, bracing his back feet into the carpet, wrapped his front paws around the center of my body.

Get off me, you stupid Truck Trash! Don't you even know the difference between a dog and a cat?!

I whipped around, and grabbing his front paw in my mouth, dug all four of my sharp incisors into his flesh. He yelped in surprise, jumped away and ran for cover. I lay down and contentedly licked the fur covering my ribs. Round one for Sakie!

Round one quickly became round two and three and four with me about to be KO'd. He was determined to murder me in my tracks. He ate my food. He drank my water. Whenever he saw me, it was a chase to the finish. With a loud snort and quick sharp bark, he was after me. I would run for my life, usually winding up in a corner or against a wall. With one leap he was on top of me, grabbing at my fur with his paws and opening his mouth to bite off my head. Someone in the family always saved me just in time. They pulled him off and carried me to a safe place. That safe place was their bathroom. When Freeway was in the house, my food and water were moved into the bathroom where I, once a princess and mistress of the house, was confined as a prisoner. The only time I was allowed into the rest of the house was when he was out with *dad*. The minute they returned, he headed straight for "the cat". I screamed. I hissed. I yowled. I was beginning to lose my confidence. At first, I believed he wouldn't really kill me, and then I was sure he would. He was so dumb he truly didn't know the difference between a family pet and a rabbit or raccoon in the woods.

The truth of it was that behind his bravado was a coward. The first time I saw him run from something was when he was confronted by a bobcat out in the grove. It was the same bobcat responsible for our two missing wild brown rabbits that Freeway had once had such pleasure chasing. On that almost fateful night, as he scampered out to the grove looking like he owned the place, he stopped dead in his tracks. Lurking between the orange trees was a spotted bobcat waiting to seize its prey. Freeway zipped his little body around and high-tailed it through the woods into the safety of the garage as fast as a streak of lightning. Then there was the time a large hungry hawk spotted him running in the field and swooped down to survey his weight. *Mom* was driving the golf cart in the distance and saw the big bird about to attack. She screamed and hit the horn while pushing the accelerator to the floorboard. The hawk flew off. Freeway jumped into the golf cart and up onto her lap, his whole body shaking. He would not go outside for three days without a member of the family to protect him.

And, since I'm at it, I may as well relate how ridiculous he looks whenever it's about to storm and he hears thunder rolling in. He becomes absolutely terrified, running around in circles and lunging at every window in the house while barking at the top of his lungs.

You are such a big baby. If you think you're going to scare the storm away with your obnoxious voice, you have another think coming.

Actually I felt a bit sorry for him because I knew that some animals have a hearing sensitivity that causes real pain from certain loud or high pitched sounds. No reassurance or distraction helps. The stupid idiot thought that he could make it go away if he attacked it.

"Love bears all things, believes all things, hopes all things, endures all things. Love never fails."
— Corinthians 1, chapter 13

Truce

W<small>E WERE STILL TRAVELING BACK</small> and forth to
Miami, but now there were four of us. When they tried to put
us both in the car Freeway went out of control. He barked and
jumped at me without manners or mercy. They put him into a
travel dog cage and I climbed into my seat between them. He
absolutely went wild, barking and clawing at the wire until I
thought his paws would bleed.

"We're sorry, Sakie," said *dad*. He opened the cage and
Freeway jumped out. Mom picked me up and put me into it
and locked the wire door.

> *This isn't fair. I was here first. I'm royalty. I'm a
> princess. He's a mutt, and he's taking my place. I
> hate him. I absolutely hate him.*

They weren't listening. Freeway curled into my center seat
and went to sleep.

When we arrived in Miami, *mom* carried me all the way
into the apartment while Freeway scampered free, leaping up
to nip at my hanging legs. She set me down in the second
bedroom and closed the door. Once again, I was only allowed
out when Freeway was not around. When he returned, it was
the same as our country house. Zoom! He chased me back into
the bedroom. As soon as he knew I was in my prison, he turned
around and acted like a darling sweet playful puppy. It got so

they didn't even have to close the door. He wasn't coming in and I wasn't going out. They only secured my safety when they left us alone. This nightmare went on for almost one year.

One afternoon they went out and forgot to close the bedroom door. I waited to be mutilated. I waited over one hour and then became curious. Where was Freeway? I tiptoed into the living room and into the kitchen where I took a drink from his water dish. In one second he was behind me. But he didn't attack me. He drank every drop of his water so I couldn't have any. Now if that wasn't rude, I didn't know what was. I was about to make a dash into the second bedroom when he whipped his head around and, with his mouth splashing bowl water, suddenly stuck out his red tongue and slurped my nose.

Ugghk! Puppy Spit, I meowed. But, he didn't appear to notice my insult. He slurped my nose, my eyes and even my ears. I sat down and purred. We walked into the living room and curled up on the sofa, back to back. And that's how *mom* and *dad* found us.

"If animals could speak, the dog would be a blundering outspoken fellow but the cat would have the rare grace of never saying a word too much."
— Mark Twain

Freeway the Great

HE HAS NEVER OUTGROWN BEING a puppy. At four years of age, he still looks like a puppy. He becomes absolutely hysterical with joy when anyone arrives. From family members to the mailman, gardener, and pool person, you would think he just found his long lost soul mate. I suspect that if a burglar broke into the house, Freeway would slurp him to death. He hasn't learned one lesson of refinement from the family or me, no matter how hard we have tried to teach him. He continues to have the worst manners imaginable. When he drinks from his dish in the kitchen, he splashes water in all directions. Then he fills his mouth and lets the water slop across the kitchen floor, creating hazardous puddles as he races away to his next adventure. On an average of once a week that new adventure combines chasing squirrels (he has yet to come close to nabbing one), carting buckets of mud and sticky green leaves into the house or, most disgusting of all, rolling in coon dung. Fortunately, he's aware of this last irresponsible behavior and sits at the back door until someone dumps him into the laundry sink to be scrubbed.

The scruffy shag-ball has everyone catering to his slightest whim. With total indiscretion, he greets family, friends, and strangers with his wildly wagging tail and a million slurps. He is so spoiled that I cannot stand to watch his antics. He started out with a tennis ball and a stuffed bear they called his 'baby'. Dad's friend, Jim, brought him a huge stuffed gray mouse we called his "Jim-toy". Susan brought a pink bunny, another friend gave him 'Miss Piggy', and dad bought him another bear for Christmas. Somehow he acquired a slipper, a Frisbee, and a curled rope with a handle on one end for a human to hold so he could pull the rope with his teeth. He has two baskets filled with all his junk, but they're always empty because his toys are scattered all over the house. Every night *mom* and *dad* gather them up and return them to the baskets, and every morning he takes them out one by one, until they're all over the place again. The brat is totally oral-fixated. He cannot enter a room without something hanging out of his mouth. The tennis ball is his favorite. He walks around all day with it so deeply submerged within his jaws that I have considered running into him so he will swallow it and choke to death. When he has forgotten where it is, he becomes frantic. Everyone says, "Freeway, go get your ball". He runs around in circles and up and down the stairs and into the dining room in mad pursuit. "Look in your basket in the bedroom," they say, and he races to the back bedroom where he finds it and marches back proudly for everyone to comment how brilliant he is.

I had had enough! *Freeway, I said, you have too many toys. You're an imprudent, spoiled mutt. You don't even know where they are half the time.*

Not true, you super-perfect snotty feline! I know every toy. I have my ball, my bear, my Jim toy, my Susan bunny, my gray mouse, Miss Piggy and dad's Christmas bear. And I know what 'imprudent' means. You're just mad because Sam

*buried your toys in the garden and you can't do
the same to mine!*

Grabbing his bear baby in his mouth, he ran to see who
was ringing the doorbell. I jolted up in astonishment. How
did he know that Sam buried my toys?

"Neither need you tell me," said Candide, "that we must take care of our garden." "You are in the right," said Pangloss; "for when man was put into the Garden of Eden, it was with an intent to dress it: and this proves that man was not born to be idle." "Work then without disputing," said Martin; "it is the only way to render life supportable."
— Voltaire Candide, 1759

My Grove

THE ONLY TIME I WAS allowed outside was when we drove in the golf cart to revel in the miracle of our beautiful citrus grove. The land had been deserted since the central Florida orange industry came to a halt from freezing temperatures throughout the 1980s. Some farmers relocated near West Palm Beach. The lucky ones sold their acreage for housing developments and conglomerates like Walmart, Publix, and Target, that plowed down healthy trees as well as all semblance of greenery on scenic Highway 441 to build huge colorless bleak buildings for the growing population to do their shopping. When we heard that a developer was about to purchase the ten acres adjacent to our property, our decision was quick and final. A bald eagle had just given birth at the top of the tallest tree. There were fat, nervy raccoons and ugly opossums and armadillos that bore holes everywhere, as well as a stunning resident red fox and one marvelous gopher turtle that Freeway had somehow made friends with. We did not tell anyone about the five foot Blue Indigo snake that showed up in our garage on occasion for fear it would be taken away or killed. No one was going to slap up cookie-cutter houses on the land that belonged to God's four-legged people.

Two years later orange and tangerine and kumquat and grapefruit blossoms filled the air with perfume, followed by tiny marbles of green fruit. By January, *mom* was squeezing and cutting and food processing. Pots of marmalade overflowed on the stove and counters, leaving a happy, gooey residue on everything. Meyer Lemons became lemon curd. Juice from Ponderosa lemons was frozen for future lemon meringue pies and the outside skin peeled for *Limoncello Liqueur.* Hundreds of Key limes from the new cold tolerant trees were turned into pound cakes and pies, with bags of extras frozen whole for the summer months. Our very favorite trees were the Meiwa round kumquats. They were completely different from the oval shaped kumquats known as Nagami. The Nagami were bitter, whereas the Meiwa could be eaten directly from the tree. Even Freeway and I ate these succulent little round morsels and we never became ill. Mixed with the Murcott and Robinson tangerines, they made incredible marmalade. Cooked in rum, Gr. Marnier and crystallized ginger, they complimented everything from duck to ice cream.

I thought I would miss the cars passing in front of our house and the roar of engines from speedboats pulling water-skiers through their wake in Biscayne Bay in the back but I hardly think of the city any more. The quietude of the gigantic oak trees and euphoric scent from our citrus grove has enveloped me in tranquility. I have become a country cat.

This is definitely the best life I have ever known.

Gifts from My Grove
Orange - Tangerine Marmalade
Yield: Approximately 8 half-pint jars

½ cup thinly slivered orange rind

3 cups total cut up orange or tangerine pulp or a combination of both

2 cinnamon sticks, broken in as many pieces as possible

2 tablespoons Gr. Marnier or orange liqueur

1 package pectin (SureJell®)

5-6 cups granulated sugar, depending upon the sweetness of the oranges

1. Combine the orange rind, oranges (tangerines) and their juice with cinnamon sticks in a large soup pot. Stir in 1 cup of the sugar. Stir and allow the mixture to stand 30 minutes.
2. Bring to a boil. Lower heat to medium and cook, stirring often, 10 minutes.
3. Return the temperature to high. Add the liqueur. Stir in the pectin. Continue stirring until mixture reaches a full boil. Pour in the remaining sugar all at once, stirring constantly. When it returns to a full boil, let it boil exactly 1 minute, stirring constantly. Remove from heat immediately. Stir and fill sterilized jars according to the directions on the pectin box.
4. Seal the jars tightly and invert them (turn upside down) for 10 minutes. Turn right-side up.
5. Label the jars with the date. The shelf life in a cool place should be up to one year.

Kumquat – Ginger Marmalade
Yield: 6 eight-ounce jars

The Nagami oval kumquat requires 2 cups more sugar than the round Meiwa kumquat.
Note that this marmalade is made without the addition of pectin. It has a different consistency than the Orange-Tangerine Marmalade.

3 pounds ripe, firm round kumquats (Meiwa) or oval kumquats (Nagami)
4 ounces crystallized ginger, soaked 15 minutes in hot water

1 cup freshly-squeezed orange or tangerine juice
2¼ pounds granulated sugar (6 cups) for round kumquats and 8 cups for oval kumquats.
1 teaspoon cinnamon extract

1. Wash kumquats in cold water. Set in water to cover in a large pot. Bring to a boil. Boil 5 minutes, covered. Drain in a colander and rinse well under cold water. Pop the skins loose from the fruit and discard the insides.
2. Chop the ginger fine with a large chef's knife. (Crystallized ginger is too sticky to chop in a food processor.) Remove to the pot. Place kumquat skins into food processor and pulverize. Return all to the pot. Add the orange juice. Add the sugar, cinnamon and liqueur. Stir. Allow to rest 30 minutes, stirring several times.
3. Bring the mixture to a very slow boil over medium heat, stirring often. Do not turn heat to high or the mixture will burn on the bottom. Simmer gently 30 minutes, or until thick, stirring often so mixture will not stick to the bottom.

4. Fill six eight-ounce (half pint) Mason-type jars, following the instructions for washing and filling. Make sure the caps are screwed on very tightly. Push the top of the caps down with your thumb. Turn upside down for 10 minutes. Turn right-side-up to cool.

Sauce for Duck, Fish or Pork
Combine 2 cups preserves with one-quarter cup Grand Marnier, apricot or Triple Sec in a saucepan. Cook over medium heat, stirring, until smooth. Keep warm until ready to serve.

Drunken Kumquats
Yield: 4 pounds = 12 half pints

4 pounds Meiwa round
    kumquats
4 cups golden rum
3 cups granulated sugar
3 cups granulated sugar

2 cups water
1 teaspoon cinnamon extract
¼ cup Gr. Marnier or peach
    liqueur

1. Insert a small, sharp knife into the top of each kumquat and push it almost to the bottom. This creates an air pocket to create an air space so the fruit will not shrivel.
2. Cover the quats with water and bring to a boil. Pour off the water.
3. Combine the rum and 3 cups sugar and pour over the quats. Cover and let it stand several hours.
4. Combine 3 cups sugar with 2 cups water and the cinnamon extract. Bring to a boil. Reduce heat to medium and boil gently 5 minutes. Add to the kumquats.

5. Add the ginger. Bring to a boil, uncovered. Stir in the Gr. Marnier.
6. Fill sterilized jars and seal tightly. Invert the jars (turn upside down) for 10 minutes.
7. Place right-side up into a dishwasher on hot cycle. Remove after the first cycle or approximately 10 minutes. Or sterilize the old-fashioned method. Fill a large soup pot half full. Set the jars upside down into it with their caps. Bring to a boil, covered. Boil 3 minutes. Drain. The jars must be very hot when filling.

Very Berry Cello Pie
A fun combination of elderberries,
blueberries, and limoncello liqueur

½ cup elderberry juice
(from 1 ½ cups cooked
elderberries)
½ cup granulated sugar
1 envelope unflavored gelatin
¼ cup limoncello liqueur,
room temperature

1 pint heavy cream
2 cups granulated sugar
1 cup fresh blueberries,
uncooked
1 cup fresh blueberries,
uncooked
10X confectioners' sugar

1. Cook the elderberries with ½ cup sugar over lowest heat to extract juice. Push through a paint strainer or squeeze through cheesecloth to measure ½ cup juice. When juice is lukewarm, sprinkle the gelatin over. Stir slightly. When thoroughly combined, add the limoncello liqueur.
2. Whip the cream with the sugar until thick. Fold in the elderberry mixture. Fold in 1 cup blueberries.
3. Refrigerate several hours or overnight.

4. Toss remaining blueberries in confectioners' sugar and arrange on top of the pie to serve.

Key Lime Pound Cake
Persian limes may be substituted
Yield: Two 8X8X2 ½ inch loaf pans

3 cups all-purpose flour, measured after sifting
½ teaspoon salt
1 level tablespoon baking powder
1 cup (½ pound) butter
2 ½ cups granulated sugar
6 jumbo eggs
2 teaspoons grated lime peel
2 teaspoons vanilla
1 cup sour cream
½ cup Key lime juice, freshly squeezed
2 tablespoons lime juice
Sifted 10X confectioner's sugar

1. Preheat oven to 350°F.
2. Sift the flour measure 3 cups. Then, sift again with the salt and baking powder. Set aside.
3. Beat the butter and cream cheese on highest speed of an electric mixer to incorporate. Add the sugar and beat until thick and white and creamy, scraping the sides of the bowl several times. Add the eggs, one at a time, beating after each addition. Scrape the bottom and sides of the bowl with a rubber spatula.
4. Add the vanilla.

5. Reduce the speed of the mixer to medium and add the sour cream. Add the lime juice. The batter might appear to curdle. Do not worry. It will incorporate when the flour is added.
6. Add the flour mixture on low speed. Scrape the sides and bottom. Beat again. Do not over-beat or cake will become tough.
7. Pour into 2 bread loaf pans or a greased and floured 10" tube pan. Bake 50-55 minutes or until an inserted wooden skewer comes out clean.
8. While still hot, mix the confectioner's sugar with the lime juice until it forms a smooth cream. Brush heavily over the top and sides with a pastry brush. The heavier the glaze, the better.

Lemon Meringue Pie
Yield: 10 inch pie

⅔ cup cornstarch
1 ½ cup granulated sugar
¼ teaspoon salt
3 cups boiling water
7 jumbo or 8 extra large egg yolks

¾ cup freshly squeezed lemon juice or Key lime or Persian lime
Baked and cooled 10 inch pie crust

1. Sift the cornstarch with the sugar and salt into a 2 quart heavy pot or the top of a double boiler. Pour the boiling water in slowly, stirring with a wooden spoon until smooth, thick and creamy.
2. Beat the egg yolks with a whisk until blended. Slowly add some of the hot mixture to them. (This is an important

technique to keep the eggs from 'scrambling') Stir mixture back into the pot and continue to cook, stirring constantly over high heat, until very thick. Stir in lemon (lime) juice and continue stirring until mixture is thick and bubbly. Remove from the heat and cool to room temperature. Spoon into the baked pie crust and refrigerate until very cold.

Note: Although it is safer to make this filling in a double boiler, cooking time will be cut in half when cooked in a heavy pot over direct heat. Cook over medium-low or the mixture will burn on the bottom.

Meringue:

7 jumbo or 8 extra large egg whites, room temperature or warmer

⅓ cup granulated sugar

2 tablespoons cornstarch

⅛ teaspoon salt

½ teaspoon cream of tartar

1. Sift together the sugar, cornstarch and salt.
2. Beat the egg whites until foamy. Add cream of tartar. Add sugar mixture a tablespoon at a time, beating on high speed until thick and glossy, approximately 6-8 minutes.
3. Cover the entire top with the meringue, bringing it up into peaks with a spoon. Or, pipe rosettes with a fluted tube. Place under the broiler to brown.

Limoncello
(The Italian lemon liqueur popular in southern Italy)
Yield 4 cups or 750 liter bottle

2 cups vodka of choice
2 cups bottled drinking water
2 cups granulated sugar
⅛ teaspoon cinnamon extract
Wedge of lemon with rind

3 Ponderosa lemons, washed
    thoroughly to measure
½ cup slivered yellow lemon
    peel (no white)
2 cups vodka

1. Combine the water, sugar, cinnamon extract and lemon in a small saucepan. Bring to a boil. Remove from the heat. Allow it to stand 1 hour, covered.
2. With a carrot peeler, peel thin strips from the rind of the lemons. Insert them into the vodka bottle. Pour in the sugar syrup. Pour in the vodka.
3. Leave at room temperature 12 hours. Refrigerate at least 2 weeks.
4. Serve very cold sparingly after dinner as a cordial.

"What greater gift than the love of a cat?"
— Charles Dickens

Predictable Sakie

SAM WOULD BE PROUD TO know that I have become very predictable in my old age. I spend my days curled up in the oversized chair in the family room waiting for the family to join me in front of the T.V. When *mom* is in the kitchen, I sit by the sink waiting for her to share something delectable. She's into healthy Florida regional cooking this year, so my samplings range from baked fried chicken and sautéed fish with lime, garlic and pepper, to grilled Cajun polenta. She's also into alligator tail, wild turkey, wood duck and venison, all of which are quite tasty, but not as sumptuous as old fashioned boiled shrimp. Although my senses are still keen, I can no longer hop up to the sink when I smell shrimp. Instead I nuzzle *mom's* leg to let her know I'm waiting for my share.

I'm still quite good at catching baby lizards that find their way into the house, even though they move so fast that I usually only get their tails. I should like to brag that I can still yodel a good high note with mom when she sings.

My happiest time is when Christopher comes to visit. He is called Chris now. It's hard to believe that he will be sixteen. I was only two years old when he was born. Before he could even walk, he chased after me, crawling on all fours. Soon he was walking, and then running. I ran also. He ran after me. He thought he was faster than I, but the truth is, I always let him catch me. He never screamed. His voice was soft. And, when he caught me, he would just lie down and set his little head over me and gently touch my fur with his fingers. He was a different kind of baby. He was my Prince. He lay against Sam the same way. The two of us had never seen such a gentle human at such a young age. It made us wonder if some humans have old souls like us.

Cats have a natural fear of young children. Their arms and legs move too quickly and their voices are high pitched, which hurts our delicate ears. They also have an inborn sense of what aggravates us the most, such as pulling our tails and sticking their pudgy little fingers in our mouths and ears. Although babies are supposed to be sweet and innocent, without intent to hurt anyone, we cats know this to be untrue. Not too long ago we were visited by friends who brought their three year old. She sat down next to me, sweetly scratching my head. When her parents turned their backs, she put her arms around me as though to embrace in a hug. Once I was held captive, she proceeded to try to break my ribs with a strength I didn't think possible in one so young. When I yowled, and her parents scolded her, she gave me a fierce pinch and sat back and smiled innocently. With my old bones aching, I stumbled out of her reach as quickly as possible and hid under the bed where she couldn't find me.

Chris doesn't play with me any longer. Teenage boys don't play with cats. Besides, he has his own dog to play with at his house. Whenever he comes to visit I greet him and he scratches my head. I feel the bond we have together and I am happy. The last time he came he noticed that I have lost half my body weight. The tall teenager didn't express any outward emotion, but I could tell he was concerned about the seventeen year-old cat that has been part of his grandparents' household since before he was born. He picked me up awkwardly in teenage-boy fashion and carried me to the chair in front of the television where he gently patted my head. The Egyptian magic I performed in his crib almost sixteen years ago had worked. I was proud of my accomplishment. I wanted to tell him that he was still as gentle and kind as when he was a baby, but I didn't know how.

*"What sort of philosophers are we, who know absolutely
nothing about the origin and destiny of cats?"*
— Henry David Thoreau, 1817-62

The Bird

I WONDER WHAT DEATH WILL BE like. I cannot remember this part of my existence or non-existence from my past lives. I want to be. I want to exist. I cannot imagine not being.

I rationalize that it is only when I sleep that I am in darkness; nothingness. But cats are never completely asleep. Cats appear to sleep but we are always on guard. The slightest noise or movement arouses our senses and sets us into motion. Even if we do not move physically, our minds perceive all that happens around us.

Is death like sleep? I sometimes dream when I sleep. Will I dream in the darkness? Or is death a black hole where there are no dreams and no stirring and no awakening? Is death the black hole of the universe? I ponder if this will be my last life or if there are more to come. Is this how humans feel? Have I become human? Is this why they are so frightened? I try to close my eyes but I am enveloped with a frantic moment and I cannot rest. I cannot sleep yet I am not awake. If I were human, I could believe in a hereafter promised by one of the many religions mankind has pursued during the twenty-five hundred years I have known them. But they are not truly sure of this either. The multitude of faiths they have practiced assures me they are all grappling with hope of their immortality rather than their assurance of same.

The philosopher, René Descartes, wrote *"cogito ergo*

sum" (I think, therefore I am), which was intended to affirm the intuition of one's own reality and the expression of the indubitable first-person experience. This logical certification of self-conscious awareness in any form discredits skepticism and insures the indubitable certainty of one's own existence. This I believe.

Who was it who said, "We come into this world alone and leave it alone." I accept this but I want so much to have another opportunity to be with those whom I have loved and to touch and feel and smell the wonderment of being.

I think about Sam. The box with his ashes is buried in our front yard under the statue of St. Francis with a small headstone that says *Sam Bear 1975-1991*. I know that his soul is not there but it's still comforting that I will be buried next to him.

I hear a sound and look to see the little bird whapping at the window. It has grown larger in the three weeks since it first appeared. It strikes the glass with greater strength than its little body should be able to endure. Occasionally it chirps. The chirp is not a song, but a heralding of its mission.

"They believed I had the soul of a human; I believed they might someday attain the spiritual immortality of a cat."
— Sakie 2004

Epilogue

It is morning. The blinds above the Jacuzzi are open filling the bathroom with sunlight. Freeway sleeps on his pillow by the bedroom door. The closet is empty. The bird is gone. It will not return. It has taken what it came for.

SAKIE CAT
1986-2004

I seem to have loved you in numberless forms, numberless times…In life after life, in age after age, forever.
— Rabindranath Tagore, 1861-1941

Postscript
3430 CE

A VERY LARGE HAND PLACES MY tiny body into the arms of a small boy I determine to be around four years.

"Happy birthday little Axion. Say hello to your very own cat."

He lowers soft curls that surround his face to cover my head and then kisses my pink ears.

I open my eyes and look around. I am not in an Egyptian citadel fortress or French palace. Nor am I in my Mount Dora house. We are encased in a glass bubble floating in space. In the distance is the outline of earth and hundreds of planets on all sides.

Oh, Great Mother of Cats, where am I?

The human mother understands my thoughts and answers, "We are on our way to *Planet Hortus* to pick up groceries for the next week's voyage to our summer residence on *Acta-Arena Litus,* where the beaches all have white sand and transparent water and the clear air rejuvenates our bodies".

We glide easily onto a landing strip. A robotic voice whispers, *Enter,* and a door slides open to expose a million miles of cultivation. Vegetables, fruits and grains of all descriptions stretch out endlessly, swaying in the soft breeze under blue sky.

The mother looks at me and answers my next question. It has been over fourteen hundred years since my last life and I am overcome with this miracle of telepathic communication between humans and animals that has evolved.

She looks directly into my eyes and speaks with her mind instead of her voice.

"This is the planet we cultivated for food after the earth's natural resources and environment was compromised and destroyed by greed, pollution and neglect. First the people overpopulated the planet. Then they plowed down all their farmlands to build structures to live and work in. Instead of developing energy alternatives, they used what was available to them until there was none left. When it was all gone, they had a great war that leveled most of their cities.

Those who survived knew they were fighting a battle against time before pollution from the weapons of mass destruction spread from the cities to the country. They unburied time capsules with instructions to build space crafts. They built hydroponic systems to grow vegetables. They learned secrets of herbs and roots for medicine and cosmetics and the value of vegetarianism with emphasis on wheat and barley from your Egyptian ancestors."

I am beginning to learn how to communicate telepathically with this new species of human and, instead of meowing, concentrate on thought process.

How long did it take before you could accomplish interplanetary travel?

"Interplanetary travel was quite easy. Interstellar travel took five hundred years to develop. Finding friendly galaxies with planets that could sustain our form of life as earth once did was the key to our survival."

The revelation that I have been born again into such an extraordinary new world is making me very tired. I put my head down and begin to dream.

The Beginning

Recipe Index

CPSIA information can be obtained at www.ICGtesting.com
Printed in the USA
LVOW07s0341220415

435512LV00001B/1/P